Dedicated to the innovators.

PROLOGUE

Python has emerged as the North Star in the vast universe of programming, where languages and frameworks change like the moon's phases. Consistent, versatile, and brilliantly designed, it shines brightly, guiding newcomers and veterans alike through the labyrinth of code.

Python for Aspiring Programmers is not just a guide—it's an invitation. It is an invitation to immerse yourself in the art and science of programming using a language that, for over three decades, has empowered creators to build everything from simple scripts to sophisticated machine-learning models. Python's simplicity and readability have made it the preferred choice for those starting their coding journey. But don't let its simplicity deceive you; NASA, Google, and countless startups and innovators around the globe have harnessed Python's power.

Every aspiring programmer stands at the threshold of countless possibilities. Behind each line of code lies not just a function or an algorithm but a story, a solution, and, often, a revolution. This book aims to be the key that unlocks that potential, offering clarity to the beginner's confusion and fueling the passion that so often drives the world of technology forward.

Together, we'll delve deep into Python's elegant syntax, explore its vast libraries, and harness its unparalleled capabilities. Step by step, chapter by chapter, you will evolve—from writing your first Python script, marveling at the immediate gratification it offers, to constructing complex, real-world applications.

As you flip these pages, remember: every coder, from the creator of Python, Guido van Rossum, to the tech giants of Silicon Valley, started with a single line of code. In your hands lies not just a book but a journey of challenges, learning, and endless discovery.

Welcome to the world of Python. Let's begin this adventure together.

Index

CHAPTER 1

PROGRAMMING AND PYTHON

What is Programming?

Welcome to the world of programming! Before diving into Python and writing code, let's take a moment to understand what programming is all about.

Programming, at its core, is about problem-solving. It's a way to tell a computer how to perform a task by giving it a set of instructions. These instructions, known as code, are written in a programming language that the computer can understand and execute. We can create software, apps, games, websites, and more through programming. In fact, much of the technology you use every day, from your smartphone to your web browser, is the result of programming.

Just as humans communicate with each other through languages like English, Spanish, or Mandarin, we communicate with computers through programming languages. Some popular programming languages include Python, Java, C++, and JavaScript. Each language has its own syntax (rules of writing) and is suited for different types of tasks.

An algorithm is a step-by-step procedure for solving a problem. It's like a recipe in a cookbook – it tells you exactly what steps to take and in what order to reach the desired outcome. Programmers design algorithms to solve specific problems and then translate these algorithms into code.

Code is the set of instructions written in a programming language that tells a computer what to do. It's the equivalent of writing down the steps of a recipe in a language the computer can understand.

Debugging: As with any creative process, writing code often involves making mistakes. Debugging is the process of finding and fixing errors (called bugs) in the code. It's like proofreading an essay to correct typos and grammatical errors.

Execution: Once the code is written and debugged, it's time to run or execute it. Execution is the process of the computer following the instructions in the code to perform the intended task. It's like cooking a dish following the steps of a recipe.

Software: Software is a collection of code that performs specific tasks. It can be as simple as a calculator app on your phone or as complex as the operating system running on your computer. Software is the final product that users interact with, created through programming.

Why Choose Python?

Python is a high-level, general-purpose programming language that is known for its simplicity and readability. It was created by Guido van Rossum and first released in 1991. Python has become one of the most popular programming languages in the world, and it is used in a wide range of applications, from web development and data analysis to scientific computing and artificial intelligence.

As you embark on your programming journey, you may wonder why we've chosen Python as our programming language of choice. There are many programming languages available, each with its own strengths and weaknesses. However, Python has several features that make it an ideal choice for beginners, as well as for a wide range of applications.

One of Python's main selling points is its easy-to-read syntax. Python code is often described as "readable" because it resembles plain English. This means that you can focus on learning programming concepts rather than getting bogged down by complicated syntax rules. As a result, Python is one of the most recommended programming languages for beginners.

Python is a highly versatile language. It can be used to build websites, develop games, automate tasks, analyze data, and much more. Python's extensive standard library and numerous third-party packages make it easy to add functionality to your programs without having to write everything from scratch.

Python has a large and active community of users, which means that if you ever encounter a problem, you're likely to find a solution online. Websites like StackOverflow and Reddit are filled with helpful Python programmers who can answer your questions. Python's community also contributes to the language's rich ecosystem of libraries and frameworks, which are pre-written pieces of code that you can use to speed up your development process.

Python is used by many top tech companies, including Google, Facebook, and Dropbox, for a wide range of applications. Its popularity means that learning Python could open up job opportunities in a variety of fields, including web development, data analysis, artificial intelligence, and more.

Python is a cross-platform language, which means that you can run Python code on various operating systems, such as Windows, macOS, and Linux, without modification. This makes it easier to share your code with others or move your projects between different computers.

While Python is a great language for beginners, it's also powerful enough for professional development. Many startups and companies use Python to build scalable and robust applications. As you grow as a programmer, you'll find that Python's features can support more complex and ambitious projects.

Python can easily integrate with other languages like C, C++, and Java. This allows you to use existing code from other languages in your Python projects, which can save time and effort.

Python is a powerful, versatile, and user-friendly programming language that is an excellent choice for both beginners and experienced developers. Its readable syntax, active community, and wide-ranging applications make it a popular choice for various projects. Whether you're interested in web development, data science, automation, or any other field, Python is a great tool to have in your programming toolbox.

In the next chapter, we will set up your Python programming environment and write your first Python script.

The Interpreter

An interpreter is a program that reads and executes code. Unlike a compiler, which converts code into machine language all at once, an interpreter processes code line-by-line, translating each statement into machine code just before it's executed. This means that with an interpreted language, you can run your code as soon as you write it – you don't have to wait for it to compile.

Interpreters are used in various programming languages, including Python, Ruby, and JavaScript. There are pros and cons to using an interpreter instead of a compiler.

Let us now introduce you to the Python interpreter and IDLE, both of which are essential tools for your Python programming journey.

The Python Interpreter

The Python interpreter is the software that executes Python code. When you run a Python script, the interpreter reads the code line by line, interprets it, and then performs the specified actions. Essentially, it's the "brain" that understands and carries out your Python instructions.

To start the Python interpreter, simply open your computer's command prompt or terminal, type "python", and press Enter. You should see the Python version number and some additional information. You're now in the Python interactive mode, indicated by the ">>>" prompt. Here, you can type Python code directly and see the results immediately. For example, type "print('Hello, World!')" and press Enter. You should see "Hello, World!" printed on the screen.

Using the Python interpreter's interactive mode is a great way to test small snippets of code, experiment with Python features, or perform quick calculations. To exit the interactive mode, type "exit()" and press Enter.

IDLE

IDLE (Integrated Development and Learning Environment) is Python's built-in integrated development environment (IDE). It provides a user-friendly interface for writing and running

Python code. IDLE is included with the standard Python

IDLE Shell

```
IDLE Shell 3.11.3
Python 3.11.3 (v3.11.3:f3909b8bc8, Apr  4 2023, 20:12:10) [Clang 13.0.0 (clang-1
300.0.29.30)] on darwin
Type "help", "copyright", "credits" or "license()" for more information.
>>>
                                                                    Ln: 3  Col: 0
```

installation, so you don't need to install it separately.

IDLE has several features that make Python programming easier:

Shell Window: When you start IDLE, you'll see the Shell window, which is similar to the Python interactive mode. You can type Python code directly into the Shell window and see the results immediately.

Text Editor: IDLE includes a text editor for writing and saving Python scripts. To open the text editor, go to "File" and select "New File." You can type your Python code here, save the file with a ".py" extension, and run the script by pressing F5 or selecting "Run Module" from the "Run" menu.

Syntax Highlighting: IDLE's text editor highlights different parts of your code in different colors, making it easier to read and understand the code. For example, keywords are highlighted in orange, strings in green, and comments in red.

Code Completion and Call Tips: As you type, IDLE suggests code completions and provides call tips for functions, helping you write code faster and with fewer errors.

Interactive Debugger: IDLE includes a debugger that allows you to set breakpoints, step through the code line by line, and inspect variables. This is a valuable tool for finding and fixing bugs in your code.

To start IDLE, search for "IDLE" in your computer's application menu or type "idle" in the command prompt or terminal. The Python interpreter and IDLE are essential tools for Python programming. The interpreter executes Python code, while IDLE provides a user-friendly environment for writing and running code. As you progress through this book, you'll use these tools to create and test Python scripts, explore Python features, and debug your code.

What Else Can Be Used To Write Python Code

You can use several tools to write Python code, ranging from simple text editors to fully-featured Integrated Development Environments (IDEs). Here are some popular options:

Text Editors

Notepad (Windows): A simple text editor that comes pre-installed on Windows. It's suitable for writing short Python scripts but lacks features for larger projects

TextMate (macOS): A lightweight text editor for macOS with support for various programming languages, including Python.

Sublime Text: A cross-platform text editor known for its speed and user-friendly interface. It supports Python syntax highlighting and can be customized with plugins.

Visual Studio Code: A free, open-source code editor developed by Microsoft. It supports Python through extensions and offers features like code completion, debugging, and Git integration.

Atom: A free, open-source text editor developed by GitHub. It supports Python and can be customized with a wide range of plugins.

Integrated Development Environments (IDEs)

PyCharm: A powerful IDE developed by JetBrains specifically for Python. It offers features like code completion, debugging, and version control integration. It's available in both free (Community) and paid (Professional) versions.

Spyder: An open-source IDE for scientific computing with Python. It comes with features like an interactive console, variable explorer, and integrated IPython support.

Thonny: A beginner-friendly IDE for Python that's especially useful for learning and teaching programming. It comes with a built-in Python interpreter and debugger.

Notebook Environments

Jupyter Notebook: An open-source web application that allows you to create and share documents containing live Python code, equations, visualizations, and narrative text. It's widely used for data analysis and scientific research.

Google Colab: A cloud-based notebook environment that offers free access to GPUs and TPUs. It's particularly useful for machine learning and deep learning projects.

Online Platforms

Repl.it: An online IDE that supports various programming languages, including Python. It allows you to write, run, and share code in your web browser.

Glitch: An online platform for creating and hosting web applications. It supports Python and offers features like real-time collaboration and version control.

When choosing a tool for writing Python code, consider factors like your experience level, project size, and specific needs. Beginners may find text editors or simple IDEs like Thonny more accessible, while experienced developers might prefer feature-rich IDEs like PyCharm for larger projects.

In the next chapter, we'll guide you through setting up your Python programming environment, including installing Python and getting started with IDLE. Let's get ready to write some Python code!

## CHAPTER 2

SETTING UP YOUR PYTHON ENVIRONMENT

Before we dive into writing code, we need to set up your Python environment. Setting up a proper Python environment will ensure that you have the necessary tools and libraries to write, test, and execute your Python code. In this chapter, we'll guide you through the process step by step.

Installing Python

First, you need to install Python on your computer. Visit the official Python website at https://www.python.org/downloads/ and download the latest version of Python for your operating system (Windows, macOS, or Linux). Run the installer and follow the on-screen instructions. Make sure to check the option "Add Python to PATH" during the installation process. Once installed, open a terminal or command prompt and type python --version to verify the installation.

Choosing an Integrated Development Environment (IDE)

While you can write Python code in any text editor, using an Integrated Development Environment (IDE) will make your life easier. IDEs provide features such as syntax highlighting, code completion, and debugging tools. Popular IDEs for Python include PyCharm, Visual Studio Code, and Atom. Choose one that suits your preferences and install it.

Setting Up a Virtual Environment

Virtual environments allow you to create isolated Python environments for your projects. This helps prevent conflicts between libraries and ensures that your projects have their own dependencies. To create a virtual environment, open a terminal or command prompt, navigate to your project folder, and run the following command:

```
python -m venv myenv
```

This will create a virtual environment named "myenv" in your project folder. To activate the virtual environment, run the following command:

On Windows:

```
myenv\Scripts\activate
```

On macOS/Linux:

```
source myenv/bin/activate
```

Installing Libraries

Python has a rich ecosystem of libraries that you can use in your projects. To install a library, use the pip tool. For example, to install the popular data analysis library Pandas, run the following command:

```
pip install pandas
```

This will install Pandas and its dependencies in your virtual environment.

Writing and Running Python Code

Open your chosen IDE and create a new Python file in your project folder. Write some Python code, such as

```python
print("Hello, Python!")
```

Save the file and run it in your IDE or terminal. If everything is set up correctly, you should see the output "Hello, Python!" in the terminal.

Managing Project Dependencies

To keep track of the libraries used in your project, create a requirements.txt file in your project folder. List the libraries and their versions, one per line. To generate this file automatically, run the following command:

```
pip freeze > requirements.txt
```

This will create a requirements.txt file with the current versions of the libraries in your virtual environment. You can use this file to recreate the environment on another computer by running the command:

```
pip install -r requirements.txt
```

Version Control: It's a good practice to use a version control system like Git to track changes in your code. Create a repository for your project on a platform like GitHub or Bitbucket, and use Git commands to commit, push, and pull changes.

Setting up your Python environment might seem like a lot of work, but it's a crucial step that will save you time and headaches in the long run. By following the steps outlined in this chapter, you'll have a solid foundation for your Python projects, ensuring that you can focus on writing code and building awesome applications. Happy coding!

## CHAPTER 3

BASIC SYNTAX AND VARIABLES

Programming languages, like human languages, have a specific structure and set of rules that dictate how programs are written and executed. In Python, these rules are referred to as syntax. Let's start with the basics of Python syntax and then move on to variables, which are essential components of any programming language.

Basic Python Syntax

Indentation Indentation refers to the spaces or tabs at the beginning of a line of code. In Python, indentation is crucial as it indicates a block of code. In many programming languages, curly braces {} are used to denote a code block, but Python uses indentation.

For example, in a simple if statement:

```python
if 5 > 2:
    print("Five is greater than two.")
```

The print() function is indented, so it's part of the if statement block. If it weren't indented, it would be outside the if statement, and the code would produce an error.

1.2 Comments Comments are lines in your code that are not executed by the interpreter. They are used to explain the code or to prevent certain lines from being executed without removing them. In Python, comments are created using the # symbol.

```python
# This is a comment
print("Hello, world!") # This is also a comment
```

In Python, you can also create multi-line comments using triple quotes (single ''' or double """). These comments can span multiple lines, and the interpreter will ignore everything between the triple quotes.

```python
'''
This is a multi-line comment.
It spans multiple lines.
'''

print("Hello, world!")
```

1.3 Statements A statement is a single line of code that performs a specific action. In Python, you don't need to end a statement with a semicolon ; (unlike in some other programming languages).

```python
x = 5
y = "Hello"
```

2. Variables

A variable in Python is like a container that stores a value. You can think of it as a label that you assign to something, so you can reference it later. Variables are used to store information that can be referenced and manipulated in a program.

2.2 Variable Names Variable names can be short (like x or y) or more descriptive (like age, total_volume, first_name). There are some rules for variable names:

- They must start with a letter or an underscore (_), not a number.
- They can only contain alpha-numeric characters and underscores (A-z, 0-9, and _).
- They are case-sensitive (age, Age, and AGE are different variables).

Variable Types

Python has several built-in types of variables, each with its specific characteristics and operations. Here are the most common ones:

Integers (int):

The integer variable type, commonly referred to as int in programming languages like Python, is used to represent whole numbers. In mathematics, whole numbers are a subset of the real numbers that do not have a fractional or decimal component. This means that integers can represent numbers like -3, -2, -1, 0, 1, 2, 3, and so on, but not numbers like 0.5, 1.3, or -2.8.

In Python, an integer is created by simply assigning a whole number to a variable without any decimal point. For example:

```
x = 5
y = -10
z = 0
```

In the above code, x, y, and z are all variables that store integers.
Integers can be used in a variety of arithmetic operations, such as addition, subtraction, multiplication, and division. Here are some examples:

```python
a = 5
b = 2
sum = a + b  # Addition
diff = a - b  # Subtraction
prod = a * b  # Multiplication
quot = a // b # Integer Division
```

Note that there are two types of division in Python: normal division (using /) and integer division (using //). Normal division will always return a float, even if the result is a whole number, while integer division will return an integer, truncating any decimal portion.

In Python, integers have no fixed size and can grow as large as the available memory allows. However, in many other programming languages, integers have a fixed size (usually 32 or 64 bits), and their value can't exceed a certain limit.

Floating-point Numbers (float):

Floating-point numbers (or simply "floats") are used to represent real numbers, which can have both whole and fractional parts. Floats are essential for performing mathematical operations that involve non-integer values.

A floating-point number is composed of two main components: the mantissa and the exponent. The mantissa is the actual digits of the number, while the exponent indicates the position of the decimal point. In scientific notation, this is expressed as: mantissa x $10^{exponent}$.

For example, the number 1234.56 can be represented in scientific notation as 1.23456×10^3, where the mantissa is 1.23456, and the exponent is 3.

In Python, you can define a floating-point number simply by including a decimal point when assigning a value to a variable. For example:

```python
x = 3.14
y = -0.5
z = 2.0
```

In the above code, x, y, and z are all variables that store floating-point numbers.

You can perform arithmetic operations with floating-point numbers, such as addition, subtraction, multiplication, and division. Here are some examples:

```python
a = 5.0
b = 2.0
sum = a + b   # Addition
diff = a - b  # Subtraction
prod = a * b  # Multiplication
quot = a / b  # Division
```

Note that division between two floating-point numbers will always result in another floating-point number, even if the division is exact. For example, 4.0 / 2.0 will yield 2.0 as a float, not 2 as an integer.

It's important to understand that floating-point numbers in computers are approximations of real numbers due to limitations in memory and processing. This can lead to some inaccuracies when performing operations with floats. For example, 0.1 + 0.2 in Python will result in 0.30000000000000004, not 0.3.

These small inaccuracies are a result of the way computers represent floating-point numbers using binary digits (bits). Not all real numbers can be exactly represented with a finite number of bits, so some rounding errors occur. This is a fundamental limitation of computers and is something to be aware of when working with floating-point numbers.

Strings (str):

A string is a sequence of characters enclosed within quotes. Strings can include letters, numbers, special characters, and even spaces. They are an essential data type used for text representation and manipulation in Python programming.

To create a string in Python, you simply enclose a sequence of characters in either single or double quotes.

```python
my_string1 = 'Hello, world!'
my_string2 = "Python is great."
```

In the above code, my_string1 and my_string2 are both string variables.

Boolean (bool):

In Python, a Boolean is a data type that represents one of two possible values: True or False. Booleans are used in programming to represent the truth or falsity of a condition. They are often used in conditional statements, loops, and other control structures to determine the flow of a program.
You can create a Boolean variable by assigning the value True or False to it, like this:

```python
is_happy = True
```

```python
is_sad = False
```

In the above code, is_happy and is_sad are both Boolean variables.

Python also allows you to create Boolean values through comparison operations. These operations compare two values and return a Boolean value based on the result of the comparison. The following are the most common comparison operators:

- ==: Equal to
- !=: Not equal to
- <: Less than
- <=: Less than or equal to
- >: Greater than
- >=: Greater than or equal to

Here are some examples:

```python
x = 10
y = 5
result1 = x == y  # False, because 10 is not equal to 5
result2 = x > y   # True, because 10 is greater than 5
```

In the above code, result1 and result2 are Boolean variables.
In addition to comparison operators, Python has logical operators that operate on Boolean values:

- and: Returns True if both operands are True
- or: Returns True if at least one operand is True
- not: Returns True if the operand is False

Here are some examples:

```python
a = True
```

```python
b = False
result3 = a and b  # False, because one operand is False
result4 = a or b   # True, because at least one operand is True
result5 = not a    # False, because the operand is True
```

In the above code, result3, result4, and result5 are Boolean variables.

List (list):

A list is a collection of items that can hold multiple values, and these values can be of any data type (e.g., integers, floats, strings, etc.). Lists are ordered, mutable (can be modified), and can contain duplicate items. They are an essential and versatile data type used in Python for various programming tasks.

Here's how you can create a list in Python:

```python
fruits = ["apple", "orange", "banana", "grape"]
```

In this example, fruits is a list of strings.

Lists have several features and methods associated with them:
Accessing Elements: You can access elements in a list by index. Indexing starts at 0 for the first element.

```python
first_fruit = fruits[0]  # Result: 'apple'
```

Slicing: You can slice a list to get a sublist.

```python
sublist = fruits[1:3]  # Result: ['orange', 'banana']
```

Modifying Elements: Lists are mutable, meaning you can change their elements.

```python
fruits[1] = "kiwi"    # Now the list is ['apple', 'kiwi', 'banana', 'grape']
```

Adding Elements: You can add elements to a list using methods like append and insert.

```python
fruits.append("mango")    # Result: ['apple', 'kiwi', 'banana', 'grape', 'mango']
fruits.insert(1, "blueberry")  # Result: ['apple', 'blueberry', 'kiwi', 'banana', 'grape', 'mango']
```

Removing Elements: You can remove elements from a list using methods like remove and pop.

```python
fruits.remove("kiwi")    # Result: ['apple', 'blueberry', 'banana', 'grape', 'mango']
fruits.pop(1)  # Result: ['apple', 'banana', 'grape', 'mango']
```

Sorting Elements: You can sort the elements in a list using the sort method.

```python
fruits.sort() # Result: ['apple', 'banana', 'grape', 'mango']
```

Reversing Elements: You can reverse the elements in a list using the reverse method.

```python
fruits.reverse() # Result: ['mango', 'grape', 'banana', 'apple']
```

Nested Lists: A list can contain other lists as its elements.

```python
nested_list = [fruits, [1, 2, 3], ["a", "b", "c"]]
```

Iterating Through a List: You can iterate through the elements of a list using a for loop.

```python
for fruit in fruits:
    print(fruit)
```

Lists are a fundamental data type in Python and are widely used for tasks such as data storage, data manipulation, and iteration. Understanding how to create, modify, and manipulate lists is crucial for any Python programmer.

Tuple (tuple):

A tuple in Python is a collection of objects which are ordered and immutable. Tuples are similar to lists, but unlike lists, once you create a tuple, you cannot alter its contents - similar to string data types.

Tuples are useful when you have a collection of items that you want to group together as an ordered set that should not be modified.
You create a tuple by enclosing a comma-separated sequence of objects in parentheses ().
Here's an example of a tuple:

```python
my_tuple = (1, 2, 3, "hello", 5.0)
```

Accessing Elements: Like a list, you can access tuple items by referring to the index number, inside square brackets.

```python
```

```python
print(my_tuple[1]) # Output: 2
```

Slicing: You can return a range of elements by specifying where to start and where to end the range.

```python
print(my_tuple[1:4]) # Output: (2, 3, 'hello')
```

Looping Through a Tuple: You can loop through the tuple items by using a for loop.

```python
for item in my_tuple:
    print(item)
```

Joining Tuples: You can join two or more tuples by using the + operator.

```python
tuple1 = (1, 2, 3)
tuple2 = (4, 5, 6)
joined_tuple = tuple1 + tuple2
print(joined_tuple) # Output: (1, 2, 3, 4, 5, 6)
```

Tuple Length: You can find the length of a tuple using the len function.

```python
length = len(my_tuple) # Output: 5
```

Nested Tuples: A tuple can contain another tuple as its element.

```python
nested_tuple = (1, 2, (3, 4, 5), 6)
```

Remember that because tuples are immutable, you cannot add or remove items after the tuple is created, nor can you modify the existing items.

Dictionary (dict):

A dictionary in Python is an unordered, mutable, and indexed collection of key-value pairs. It allows you to store data in the form of key-value pairs, where each key must be unique. Dictionaries are very fast because they allow you to find values based on their keys, making it easier to organize and retrieve data.

To create a dictionary in Python, you can use curly braces {} and separate the keys and values with a colon :.

Here's an example of a dictionary:

```python
my_dict = {"name": "John", "age": 30, "city": "New York"}
```

In this example, "name", "age", and "city" are the keys, and "John", 30, and "New York" are the corresponding values.

Here are some basic operations you can perform with dictionaries:

Accessing Items: You can access an item in a dictionary by referring to its key inside square brackets.

```python
print(my_dict["name"]) # Output: John
```

Adding Items: You can add new key-value pairs to a dictionary.

```python
my_dict["profession"] = "Engineer" # Adds a new key-value
pair to the dictionary
```

Modifying Items: You can modify the value of an existing key by referring to the key.

```python
my_dict["age"] = 35 # Changes the value of the key "age" to
35
```

Removing Items: You can remove items from a dictionary using the del statement or the pop() method.

```python
del my_dict["city"] # Removes the key "city" and its value
my_dict.pop("age") # Removes the key "age" and its value
```

Iterating Through a Dictionary: You can loop through a dictionary using a for loop.

```python
for key, value in my_dict.items():
    print(key, value)
```

Checking If a Key Exists: You can check if a specific key exists in the dictionary.

```python
if "name" in my_dict:
    print("Name exists in the dictionary")
```

Dictionary Length: You can find the length of a dictionary using the len function.

```python
```

```python
length = len(my_dict) # Returns the number of key-value pairs
in the dictionary
```

Nested Dictionaries: A dictionary can contain another dictionary as its value.

```python
nested_dict = {"person": {"name": "John", "age": 30},
"location": {"city": "New York", "country": "USA"}}
```

Dictionaries are a powerful data type in Python and are widely used to store and organize data, especially when you want to access the data based on specific keys. Understanding how to create, modify, and manipulate dictionaries is essential for any Python programmer.

Set (set): A set in Python is an unordered collection of unique elements. It is similar to a list or a dictionary, but unlike a list, it doesn't allow duplicate elements, and unlike a dict onary, it doesn't use key-value pairs. Sets are very efficient when you need to check whether a specific item exists in a collection or not, and they also support mathematical operations like union, intersection, difference, and symmetric difference.
To create a set in Python, you can use curly braces {} and separate the elements with commas, or you can use the set() constructor.

```python
my_set = {1, 2, 3, 4, 5}
my_set = set([1, 2, 3, 4, 5])
```

Here are some basic operations you can perform with sets:

Adding Items: You can add a single item to a set using the add() method, or you can add multiple items using the update() method.

```python
my_set.add(6) # Adds the element 6 to the set
my_set.update([7, 8, 9]) # Adds the elements 7, 8, and 9 to the
set
```

Removing Items: You can remove an item from a set using the remove() or discard() methods.

```python
my_set.remove(3) # Removes the element 3 from the set
my_set.discard(4) # Removes the element 4 from the set
```

Set Operations: Sets support various mathematical operations.

Union: Returns a set that contains all the elements from two sets.

```python
set1 = {1, 2, 3}
set2 = {3, 4, 5}
union_set = set1.union(set2)
print(union_set) # Output: {1, 2, 3, 4, 5}
```

Intersection: Returns a set that contains only the elements that are common to both sets.

```python
intersection_set = set1.intersection(set2)
print(intersection_set) # Output: {3}
```

Difference: Returns a set that contains the elements that are in one set but not in another.

```python
difference_set = set1.difference(set2)
```

```python
print(difference_set) # Output: {1, 2}
```

Symmetric Difference: Returns a set that contains the elements that are in either set but not in both.

```python
symmetric_difference_set = set1.symmetric_difference(set2)
print(symmetric_difference_set) # Output: {1, 2, 4, 5}
```

Set Length: You can find the length of a set using the len function.

```python
length = len(my_set)
```

Looping Through a Set: You can loop through the elements of a set using a for loop.

```python
for item in my_set:
    print(item)
```

Remember that sets are unordered collections, so when you loop through a set or display its elements, the order may be different every time you run the code.

Variable Type Checking and Conversion

You can check a variable's type using the type() function.

```python
x = 5
print(type(x)) # Output: <class 'int'>
```

To convert between types, you can use functions like int(), float(), and str().

```python
x = 5.5
y = int(x)        # y is now an integer with a value of 5
z = str(x)        # z is now a string with a value of "5.5"
```

It's essential to have a solid grasp of Python's syntax rules and variables as you continue learning and experimenting with the language. Understanding these fundamental concepts will make it easier to read and write more complex Python programs

Assigning a Variable To assign a value to a variable, use the equals sign =. The variable name goes on the left of the equals sign, and the value you want to assign goes on the right.

```python
x = 5
y = "Hello, world!"
```

## CHAPTER 4

STRINGS AND TEXT MANIPULATION

Strings are a fundamental data type in Python used to represent textual data. In Python, strings are objects that store sequences of characters. This chapter will delve into various methods for manipulating and working with strings in Python.

Creating Strings

In Python, you can create a string by enclosing characters in single or double quotes.

```python
single_quotes = 'Hello, World!'
double_quotes = "Hello, World!"
```

For multi-line strings, you can use triple quotes (either single or double).

```python
multi_line_string = '''This is a multi-line string.
It spans multiple lines.
It is very useful for large chunks of text.'''
```

Accessing Characters in a String

Python allows you to access individual characters of a string using indexing. Remember, indexing starts from 0.

```python
my_string = "Hello, World!"
print(my_string[0])  # Output: H
```

You can also use negative indexing to access characters from the end of the string.

```python
print(my_string[-1])  # Output: !
```

Slicing Strings

You can use the slice notation to get a substring from a string.

```python
my_string = "Hello, World!"
substring = my_string[0:5]
print(substring)  # Output: Hello
```

In the slice notation, the first number is the starting index, the second number is the stopping index, and the third number (optional) is the step.

String Concatenation

You can use the + operator to concatenate strings.

```python
first_name = "John"
last_name = "Doe"
full_name = first_name + " " + last_name
print(full_name)  # Output: John Doe
```

String Formatting

Python provides various ways to format strings. One common method is using the format() function.

```python
name = "John"
age = 30
formatted_string = "My name is {} and I am {} years old.".format(name, age)
```

```python
print(formatted_string)
```

In Python 3.6+, you can use f-strings for string formatting.

```python
formatted_string = f"My name is {name} and I am {age} years old."
print(formatted_string)
```

Common String Methods

Python provides many methods for manipulating strings. Some commonly used methods are:

- lower(): Converts a string to lowercase.
- upper(): Converts a string to uppercase.
- replace(old, new): Replaces occurrences of the old substring with the new substring.
- split(separator): Splits a string into a list of substrings using a separator.
- strip(): Removes whitespace from the beginning and end of a string.
- find(substring): Returnspages the index of the first occurrence of a substring. Returns -1 if not found.

Example:

```python
my_string = "  Hello, World!   "
print(my_string.lower())       # Output:   hello, world!
print(my_string.upper())       # Output:   HELLO, WORLD!
print(my_string.replace('o', 'a')) # Output:  Halla, Warld!
print(my_string.split(','))    # Output: ['  Hello', ' World!   ']
print(my_string.strip())       # Output: Hello, World!
print(my_string.find('W'))     # Output: 10
```

7. Checking String Properties

You can use various methods to check specific properties of strings.

- isdigit(): Checks if the string consists of digits.
- isalpha(): Checks if the string consists of alphabetic characters.
- islower(): Checks if the string is in lowercase.
- isupper(): Checks if the string is in uppercase.
- startswith(substring): Checks if the string starts with a specific substring.
- endswith(substring): Checks if the string ends with a specific substring.

python
```python
my_string = "Hello123"
print(my_string.isdigit())        # Output: False
print(my_string.isalpha())        # Output: False
print(my_string.islower())        # Output: False
print(my_string.isupper())        # Output: False
print(my_string.startswith('H')) # Output: True
print(my_string.endswith('3'))  # Output: True
```

8. Escape Characters

In strings, you can use escape characters to include special characters, like newline (\n) and tab (\t).

python
```python
escaped_string = "Hello,\nWorld!\tHow are you?"
print(escaped_string)
```

9. Raw Strings

You can use raw strings to ignore escape characters. Raw strings are prefixed with r.

```python
raw_string = r"Hello,\nWorld!\tHow are you?"
print(raw_string)  # Output: Hello,\nWorld!\tHow are you?
```

10. String Length

You can use the len() function to get the length of a string.

```python
my_string = "Hello, World!"
length = len(my_string)
print(length)  # Output: 13
```

## CHAPTER 5

WORKING WITH NUMBERS

Working with numbers is a fundamental skill in programming. In Python, there are several types of numbers and a wide array of operations that can be performed with them. This chapter will explore the different numerical types, arithmetic operations, and functions in Python.

Numerical Types

There are four numerical types in Python: int, float, complex, and bool.

Integer Type ('int')

In Python, the integer type is represented by the keyword 'int'. Integers are whole numbers that can be either positive or negative, including zero. They are one of the most basic and commonly used data types in Python, as they are essential for mathematical and logical operations.

Defining Integers

You can define an integer by simply assigning a whole number to a variable. In Python, the '=' symbol is used for assignment.

```python
x = 10
y = -5
z = 0
```

In this example, x, y, and z are variables, and 10, -5, and 0 are integers.

Arithmetic Operations with Integers

Python supports a wide range of arithmetic operations with integers. Here are some of the most common ones:

- **Addition: 3 + 2** results in **5**
- **Subtraction: 3 - 2** results in **1**
- **Multiplication: 3 * 2** results in **6**
- **Division: 3 / 2** results in **1.5** (note: this returns a float, not an int)
- **Floor Division: 3 // 2** results in **1**
- **Modulus: 3 % 2** results in **1** (returns the remainder of the division)
- **Exponentiation: 3 ** 2** results in **9** (3 raised to the power of 2)

Converting to Integer

You can convert other data types to integer using the int() function. This is particularly useful for converting floats or strings to integers.

```python
a = int(3.14)  # Converts the float 3.14 to the integer 3
b = int("10")  # Converts the string "10" to the integer 10
```

Converts the string "10" to the integer 10
Note: The int() function will truncate (not round) any decimal places when converting from a float.

Base Representation

By default, Python uses base-10 (decimal) for integers. However, you can represent integers in other bases, such as binary (base-2), octal (base-8), or hexadecimal (base-16).

```python
binary_num = 0b1010   # Binary representation, equivalent to 10 in decimal
octal_num = 0o12      # Octal representation, equivalent to 10 in decimal
hex_num = 0xA         # Hexadecimal representation, equivalent to 10 in decimal
```

You can also convert integers to different bases using functions like bin(), oct(), and hex().

Limitations of Integers

In Python, integers can be arbitrarily large, limited only by the available memory of your computer. In other words, Python does not have a maximum integer value, and it will automatically handle large integers for you.

```python
large_int = 1234567890123456789012345678 90
```

Floating Point Type ('float')

Floating-point numbers (or 'floats') are real numbers that have a decimal point. They can represent both integer and fractional parts and can be either positive or negative. In Python, the 'float' type is used to represent these numbers. Floating-point numbers are essential for representing real-world quantities that aren't whole numbers, like measurements or probabilities.

Defining Floats

You can define a float by simply assigning a number with a decimal point to a variable.

```python
x = 3.14
y = -0.5
z = 2.0
```

In this example, x, y, and z are variables, and 3.14, -0.5, and 2.0 are floats.

Arithmetic Operations with Floats
Python supports a variety of arithmetic operations with floats, just like with integers. Here are the most common ones:

- **Addition: 3.5 + 2.5** results in **6.0**
- **Subtraction: 3.5 - 2.5** results in **1.0**
- **Multiplication: 3.5 * 2.5** results in **8.75**
- **Division: 3.5 / 2.5** results in **1.4**

As with integers, you can also use floor division, modulus, and exponentiation with floats.

Converting to Float

You can convert other data types to float using the float() function. This is particularly useful for converting strings or integers to floats.

```python
a = float(3)     # Converts the integer 3 to the float 3.0
b = float("3.5") # Converts the string "3.5" to the float 3.5
```

Converts the string "3.5" to the float 3.5

Precision and Representation

Floating-point numbers in Python are typically represented using 64 bits in the IEEE 754 standard format, which consists of three parts: the sign bit, the exponent, and the fraction. This representation allows for a wide range of values but can lead to some precision issues. For example, some decimal numbers can't be exactly represented as binary fractions, which can lead to rounding errors.

```python
result = 0.1 + 0.2
print(result)  # Outputs: 0.30000000000000004
```

In this example, the sum of 0.1 and 0.2 is not exactly 0.3 due to the way floating-point numbers are represented in binary.

Comparing Floats

Due to the aforementioned precision issues, comparing floats for equality can be tricky. Instead of directly comparing two floats, it's often better to use a small tolerance value.

```python
a = 0.1 + 0.2
b = 0.3
tolerance = 1e-9
if abs(a - b) < tolerance:
    print("The numbers are close enough.")
```

In this example, we're checking if the absolute difference between a and b is smaller than a tiny tolerance value, which indicates that the numbers are close enough to be considered equal.

Complex Numbers

Complex numbers are numbers that have both a real part and an imaginary part. They are used extensively in mathematics, physics, and engineering. In Python, you can use the complex type to work with complex numbers.

Defining Complex Numbers

You can define a complex number by using the complex() function or by using the j notation for the imaginary part.

```python
a = complex(1, 2)  # Defines a complex number with real part 1 and imaginary part 2
b = 3 + 4j         # Another way to define a complex number
```

In this example, a and b are complex numbers. a has a real part of 1 and an imaginary part of 2. b has a real part of 3 and an imaginary part of 4.

Accessing the Real and Imaginary Parts

You can access the real and imaginary parts of a complex number using the real and imag attributes.

```python
c = 5 + 6j
real_part = c.real  # Gets the real part, which is 5
imag_part = c.imag  # Gets the imaginary part, which is 6
```

In this example, c is a complex number, and we're accessing its real and imaginary parts.

Arithmetic Operations with Complex Numbers

You can perform arithmetic operations with complex numbers just like with real numbers.

- Addition: **(1 + 2j) + (3 + 4j)** results in **(4 + 6j)**
- Subtraction: **(1 + 2j) - (3 + 4j)** results in (-2 - 2j)
- **Multiplication**: **(1 + 2j) * (3 + 4j)** results in **(-5 + 10j)**
- **Division**: **(1 + 2j) / (3 + 4j)** results in **(0.44 + 0.08j)**

Complex Conjugate

The complex conjugate of a complex number is obtained by changing the sign of its imaginary part. The conjugate() method returns the complex conjugate.

```python
d = 7 + 8j
e = d.conjugate()  # Gets the complex conjugate, which is (7 - 8j)
```

In this example, d is a complex number, and e is its complex conjugate.

Absolute Value of a Complex Number

The absolute value of a complex number is the distance from the origin to the point representing the complex number in the complex plane. You can use the abs() function to get the absolute value.

```python
f = 9 + 12j
g = abs(f)  # Gets the absolute value, which is 15.0
```

In this example, f is a complex number, and g is its absolute value.

Polar Form of a Complex Number

Complex numbers can also be represented in polar form, which consists of a magnitude and an angle (or phase). You can use the cmath module to convert a complex number to polar form.

```python
import cmath
h = 10 + 10j
magnitude, phase = cmath.polar(h)
```

In this example, h is a complex number, and we're getting its magnitude and phase.

Complex numbers are a powerful tool in Python, especially for solving problems in fields like mathematics, physics, and engineering. They extend the real numbers by adding an imaginary part, allowing for a richer set of mathematical operations and concepts

Boolean Data Type

In Python, the Boolean data type allows you to work with two truth values: **True** and **False**. Booleans are often used in conditional statements, loops, and other places where a truth value is required. In Python, the Boolean data type is known as bool.

Defining Boolean Values

You can define a Boolean value by using the keywords True and False, with the initial letter capitalized.

```python
a = True
b = False
```

In this example, a is a Boolean value that is true, and b is a Boolean value that is false.

Logical Operators

You can use logical operators to combine Boolean values. The three main logical operators are and, or, and not.

- **and**: Returns True if both operands are True.
- **or**: Returns True if at least one of the operands is True.
- **not**: Returns True if the operand is False, and False if the operand is True.

```python
c = True and False  # Returns False
d = True or False   # Returns True
e = not True        # Returns False
```

In this example, c, d, and e are Boolean values that result from the use of logical operators.

Comparison Operators

Comparison operators return a Boolean value based on the relationship between two operands.

- ==: Returns True if the operands are equal.
- !=: Returns True if the operands are not equal.
- <: Returns True if the left operand is less than the right operand.
- <=: Returns True if the left operand is less than or equal to the right operand.
- >: Returns True if the left operand is greater than the right operand.
- >=: Returns True if the left operand is greater than or equal to the right operand.

```python
f = 5 == 5  # Returns True
g = 5 != 6  # Returns True
h = 5 < 6   # Returns True
```

In this example, f, g, and h are Boolean values that result from the use of comparison operators.

Implicit Type Conversion

Python sometimes automatically converts other data types to Boolean values in contexts where a truth value is expected, such as in an if statement. By default, an object is considered truthy unless its class defines a **__bool__()** method that returns False or a **__len__()** method that returns zero.

```python
i = bool(0)      # Returns False
j = bool(42)     # Returns True
k = bool("")     # Returns False
l = bool("abc")  # Returns True
```

In this example, i, j, k, and l are Boolean values that result from implicit type conversion.

Booleans are a fundamental data type in Python, and they are crucial for controlling the flow of a program. They represent the two truth values that are the basis of classical logic, and they can be combined and manipulated using logical and comparison operators.

Math Functions

Python has a built-in module named 'math' that provides a wide range of mathematical functions. To use these functions, you'll need to import the module into your program with the statement import math.

math.sqrt(x): Returns the square root of x.

python
```python
import math
result = math.sqrt(25)
print(result)  # Output: 5.0
```

math.pow(x, y): Returns x raised to the power of y.

python
```python
import math
result = math.pow(2, 3)
print(result)  # Output: 8.0
```

math.exp(x): Returns the natural exponential of x (e^x).

python
```python
import math
result = math.exp(1)
print(result)  # Output: 2.718281828459045
```

math.log(x[, base]): Returns the natural logarithm of x (base e). If the base is specified, it returns the logarithm of x to the given base.

python
```python
import math
result = math.log(100, 10)
print(result)  # Output: 2.0
```

math.sin(x): Returns the sine of x, where x is in radians.

python
```python
import math
result = math.sin(math.pi/2)
print(result)  # Output: 1.0
```

math.cos(x): Returns the cosine of x, where x is in radians.

```python
import math
result = math.cos(0)
print(result)  # Output: 1.0
```

math.tan(x): Returns the tangent of x, where x is in radians.

```python
import math
result = math.tan(math.pi/4)
print(result)  # Output: 1.0
```

math.radians(x): Converts x from degrees to radians.

```python
import math
result = math.radians(180)
print(result)  # Output: 3.141592653589793
```

math.degrees(x): Converts x from radians to degrees.

```python
import math
result = math.degrees(math.pi)
print(result)  # Output: 180.0
```

math.ceil(x): Returns the smallest integer greater than or equal to x.

```python
import math
result = math.ceil(3.2)
print(result)  # Output: 4
```

math.floor(x): Returns the largest integer less than or equal to x.

```python
import math
result = math.floor(3.8)
print(result)  # Output: 3
```

math.fabs(x): Returns the absolute value of x.

```python
import math
result = math.fabs(-5)
print(result)  # Output: 5.0
```

math.factorial(x): Returns the factorial of x.

```python
import math
result = math.factorial(5)
print(result)  # Output: 120
```

These functions are just a subset of the full range of mathematical functions available in the math module. They are essential for performing advanced mathematical computations and are widely used in scientific, engineering, and data analysis applications.

Random Numbers

Random numbers play a vital role in various fields such as cryptography, computer simulations, statistics, and gaming. In Python, the random module provides functions to generate random numbers. Below is a detailed discussion of some of the important functions in the random module:

random.random(): Returns a random float between 0 and 1.

```python
import random
result = random.random()
print(result)  # Example Output: 0.6824904066244266
```

random.uniform(a, b): Returns a random float between a and b, where a <= x <= b.

```python
import random
result = random.uniform(5, 10)
print(result)  # Example Output: 7.293902408598813
```

random.randint(a, b): Returns a random integer between a and b, including both endpoints.

```python
import random
result = random.randint(1, 6)
print(result)  # Example Output: 4
```

random.randrange(start, stop[, step]): Returns a random integer from the specified range. The range is defined by the start and stop arguments, and the step argument can be used to specify the interval between numbers in the range.

```python
import random
result = random.randrange(0, 10, 2)
print(result)  # Example Output: 8
```

random.choice(seq): Returns a random element from the given sequence.

```python
import random
fruits = ['apple', 'banana', 'cherry', 'date', 'fig']
result = random.choice(fruits)
```

```python
print(result)  # Example Output: 'cherry'
```

random.sample(population, k): Returns a list of k unique elements randomly selected from the given population.

```python
import random
numbers = [1, 2, 3, 4, 5, 6, 7, 8, 9, 10]
result = random.sample(numbers, 5)
print(result)  # Example Output: [3, 8, 2, 6, 7]
```

random.shuffle(x): Shuffles the order of elements in the given list. This function doesn't return a new list; it modifies the original list in place.

```python
import random
numbers = [1, 2, 3, 4, 5]
random.shuffle(numbers)
print(numbers)  # Example Output: [5, 3, 1, 4, 2]
```

random.seed(a=None, version=2): Initializes the random number generator with a seed value, which can be an integer, a string, or any hashable object. Providing a seed ensures that you get the same sequence of random numbers every time the random functions are called. This is useful for testing and debugging purposes.

```python
import random
random.seed(42)
print(random.random())  # Output: 0.6394267984578837
random.seed(42)
print(random.random())  # Output: 0.6394267984578837
```

These functions are just some of the most commonly used ones in the random module. There are many more functions available for generating random numbers and working with probability distributions, such as normal, exponential, and Poisson distributions. Being familiar with the various functions in the random module will enable you to create more complex and interesting Python programs that rely on randomization and probability.

Understanding how to work with numbers is crucial for any programmer. Python's built-in numerical types, arithmetic operations, and math functions make it easy to perform complex calculations and solve mathematical problems. By mastering these concepts, you'll be well-equipped to tackle a wide range of programming tasks.

## CHAPTER 6

BOOLEAN LOGIC AND CONDITIONAL STATEMENTS

Boolean logic and conditional statements are the cornerstones of any programming language, and Python is no exception. They allow you to make decisions, control the flow of your program, and perform different actions based on the conditions you set. This chapter will guide you through the principles of Boolean logic and how to use conditional statements in Python.

Boolean logic, named after mathematician George Boole, is a form of algebra where all values are reduced to either True or False, represented as 1 and 0, respectively. It is a system of logic dealing with binary variables and operations on those variables. The main Boolean operators are:

1. **AND (and)**: True if both operands are True.
2. **OR (or)**: True if at least one of the operands is True.
3. **NOT (not)**: True if the operand is False, and False if the operand is True.

Python uses the keywords and, or, and not for these operations. Here are some examples:

```python
True and True  # Output: True
True and False # Output: False
False or True  # Output: True
not True       # Output: False
```

Comparison Operators

Comparison operators are used to compare two values. The comparison operators in Python are:
1. Equal to (==)
2. Not equal to (!=)
3. Greater than (>)
4. Less than (<)
5. Greater than or equal to (>=)
6. Less than or equal to (<=)

Examples:

```python
5 == 5  # Output: True
3 != 4  # Output: True
2 > 1   # Output: True
2 < 3   # Output: True
5 >= 5  # Output: True
4 <= 3  # Output: False
```

Conditional Statements

Conditional statements allow you to execute different code based on certain conditions. Python supports three types of conditional statements: if, elif, and else.

if statement: Executes a block of code if a specified condition is True.

```python
x = 5
if x > 0:
    print("x is positive")
```

elif statement: Allows you to check multiple conditions in a single if-elif-else block. It's used after an if statement and before an else statement.

```python
x = 0
if x > 0:
    print("x is positive")
elif x < 0:
    print("x is negative")
```

else statement: Executes a block of code if none of the preceding conditions are True.

```python
x = 0
if x > 0:
    print("x is positive")
elif x < 0:
    print("x is negative")
else:
    print("x is zero")
```

You can combine multiple conditions using the and, or, and not operators.

```python
x = 15
if x > 0 and x % 5 == 0:
    print("x is a positive multiple of 5")
```

Nested If Statements

You can use an if, elif, or else statement inside another if, elif, or else statement. This is called nesting.

```python
x = 20
if x > 0:
    if x % 2 == 0:
        print("x is a positive even number")
    else:
        print("x is a positive odd number")
else:
    print("x is non-positive")
```

The Ternary Operator

The ternary operator (also called the conditional expression) allows you to return a value based on a condition in a single line of code. The syntax is:

```python
value_if_true if condition else value_if_false
```

Example:
```python
x = 5 message = "x is positive" if x > 0 else "x is non-positive"
print(message)
```

Boolean logic and conditional statements are fundamental concepts in programming. They enable you to make decisions, control the flow of your program, and create more dynamic and flexible code. In this chapter, you learned about Boolean operators, comparison operators, and various types of conditional statements. By mastering these concepts, you'll be well-equipped to tackle more complex programming tasks in Python.

CHAPTER 7
LISTS AND ARRAYS

A list is a data structure that stores multiple items in a single variable. Lists are ordered, changeable (or mutable), and allow duplicate elements.

A list is defined by enclosing a comma-separated sequence of items within square brackets [].

```python
my_list = [1, 2, 3, 4, 5]
print(my_list)  # Output: [1, 2, 3, 4, 5]
```

Lists can contain items of different data types.

```python
mixed_list = [1, 'apple', 3.14, True]
print(mixed_list)  # Output: [1, 'apple', 3.14, True]
```

Accessing Items

You can access items in a list by their index. Indexing in Python starts at 0.

```python
fruits = ['apple', 'banana', 'cherry']
print(fruits[0])  # Output: apple
print(fruits[2])  # Output: cherry
```

Negative indexing allows you to access items from the end of the list.

```python
print(fruits[-1])  # Output: cherry
```

Slicing Lists

List slicing is a technique in Python to extract a portion of a list called a slice. You can use slicing to extract elements from a list based on their positions (indices). This can be very handy when working with lists, as it allows you to extract specific sections of a list without having to iterate over the entire list.

List slicing is done using the colon (:) symbol. Here's the basic syntax:

```python
new_list = old_list[start:stop:step]
```

- start: The index of the first element in the slice. If omitted, it defaults to 0.
- stop: The index of the first element that is *not* included in the slice. If omitted, it defaults to the length of the list.
- step: The interval between elements in the slice. If omitted, it defaults to 1.

Here are a few examples:

```python
my_list = [0, 1, 2, 3, 4, 5]
```

```python
# Extract elements from index 1 to 4
print(my_list[1:5]) # Output: [1, 2, 3, 4]
# Extract elements from index 0 to 4 with a step of 2
print(my_list[0:5:2]) # Output: [0, 2, 4]
# Extract the last three elements
print(my_list[-3:]) # Output: [3, 4, 5]
```

```python
# Extract the first three elements
print(my_list[:3])  # Output: [0, 1, 2]
# Reverse the list
print(my_list[::-1])  # Output: [5, 4, 3, 2, 1, 0]
```

In the examples above, you can see how you can easily extract specific parts of a list using the colon syntax. You can omit the start, stop, or step values if they're not needed for the specific slice you want. Slicing is a very powerful tool when working with lists in Python, as it allows you to quickly and easily manipulate data without having to write extensive loops or conditions.

List Methods

append(item): Adds an item to the end of the list.
Example:

```python
fruits = ['apple', 'banana']
fruits.append('cherry')
print(fruits)  # Output: ['apple', 'banana', 'cherry']
```

insert(index, item): Inserts an item at a specified index.
Example:

```python
fruits = ['apple', 'cherry']
fruits.insert(1, 'banana')
print(fruits)  # Output: ['apple', 'banana', 'cherry']
```

extend(iterable): Adds all the elements of an iterable (list, tuple, string etc.) to the end of the list.
Example:

```python
fruits = ['apple', 'banana']
fruits.extend(['cherry', 'date'])
print(fruits)  # Output: ['apple', 'banana', 'cherry', 'date']
```

remove(item): Removes the first occurrence of the item from the list.
Example:

```python
fruits = ['apple', 'banana', 'cherry']
fruits.remove('banana')
print(fruits)  # Output: ['apple', 'cherry']
```

pop(index): Removes and returns the item at the given index. If no index is specified, it removes and returns the last item.
Example:

```python
fruits = ['apple', 'banana', 'cherry']
popped = fruits.pop(1)
print(popped)  # Output: 'banana'
print(fruits)  # Output: ['apple', 'cherry']
```

clear(): Removes all the items from the list.
Example:

```python
fruits = ['apple', 'banana', 'cherry']
fruits.clear()
print(fruits)  # Output: []
```

index(item, start, end): Returns the index of the first occurrence of the item. Optionally, start and end can be used to narrow the search.
Example:

```python
fruits = ['apple', 'banana', 'cherry', 'banana']
print(fruits.index('banana'))  # Output: 1
print(fruits.index('banana', 2))  # Output: 3
```

count(item): Returns the number of times the item appears in the list.
Example:

```python
fruits = ['apple', 'banana', 'cherry', 'banana']
print(fruits.count('banana'))  # Output: 2
```

sort(key=None, reverse=False): Sorts the items of the list. The key parameter can be used to customize the sort order, and reverse can be set to True for descending order.
Example:

```python
fruits = ['cherry', 'banana', 'apple']
fruits.sort()
print(fruits)  # Output: ['apple', 'banana', 'cherry']
```

reverse(): Reverses the order of the items in the list.
Example:

```python
fruits = ['cherry', 'banana', 'apple']
fruits.reverse()
print(fruits)  # Output: ['apple', 'banana', 'cherry']
```

copy(): Returns a shallow copy of the list.
Example:

```python
fruits = ['apple', 'banana', 'cherry']
```

```python
new_fruits = fruits.copy()
print(new_fruits)  # Output: ['apple', 'banana', 'cherry']
```

In addition to the list methods I've already explained, here are some more advanced methods you can use with Python lists:
all(): Returns True if all elements in the list are true.
Example:

```python
mylist = [True, True, True]
result = all(mylist)
print(result)  # Output: True
```

any(): Returns True if any element in the list is true.
Example:

```python
mylist = [False, True, False]
result = any(mylist)
print(result)  # Output: True
```

enumerate(): Returns an enumerate object that contains pairs of index and element for each item in the list.
Example:

```python
mylist = ['apple', 'banana', 'cherry']
result = list(enumerate(mylist))
print(result)  # Output: [(0, 'apple'), (1, 'banana'), (2, 'cherry')]
```

filter(function, iterable): Filters the elements of a list based on a function.
Example:

```python
def is_even(x):
```

```python
    return x % 2 == 0

mylist = [1, 2, 3, 4, 5]
result = list(filter(is_even, mylist))
print(result)  # Output: [2, 4]
```

map(function, iterable): Applies a function to each element of a list.
Example:

```python
def double(x):
    return x * 2
mylist = [1, 2, 3, 4, 5]
result = list(map(double, mylist))
print(result)  # Output: [2, 4, 6, 8, 10]
```

reduce(function, iterable): Applies a function of two arguments cumulatively to the elements of a list, from left to right, so as to reduce the list to a single value.
Example:

```python
from functools import reduce

def add(x, y):
    return x + y

mylist = [1, 2, 3, 4, 5]
result = reduce(add, mylist)
print(result)  # Output: 15
```

zip(*iterables): Takes two or more lists and returns an iterator of tuples, where the i-th tuple contains the i-th element from each of the input iterables.
Example:

```python
list1 = ['a', 'b', 'c']
list2 = [1, 2, 3]
result = list(zip(list1, list2))
print(result)  # Output: [('a', 1), ('b', 2), ('c', 3)]
```

Arrays

In Python, arrays are provided by the array module. Arrays are similar to lists but can only contain items of the same data type. Here's how to create an array:

```python
from array import array

arr = array('i', [1, 2, 3, 4, 5])
print(arr)  # Output: array('i', [1, 2, 3, 4, 5])
```

Arrays support most of the list operations, but are generally less flexible. However, arrays can be more efficient in terms of memory and performance for specific use cases.

## CHAPTER 8

LOOPS AND ITERATION

Iteration is the process of doing something over and over again, with a specific goal in mind. In the context of programming, iteration refers to the process of executing a set of instructions multiple times, typically using a loop.

For example, imagine you have a list of numbers and you want to add them all together. Instead of writing a separate instruction for each number, you could use a loop to iterate through the list and add each number one by one.

Here's a simple example to illustrate the concept:

Let's say you have a list of five numbers: [1, 2, 3, 4, 5]. You want to find the sum of these numbers.

Using iteration, you would start with the first number (1) and add it to a running total (which starts at 0). So, the total would become 1. Then, you would move on to the next number (2) and add it to the total, making the total 3. You would repeat this process for each number in the list, adding each one to the running total until you've gone through the entire list. At the end, the total would be 15, which is the sum of the numbers in the list.

In this example, the loop allows you to iterate through the list of numbers and perform the same action (adding the number to the total) for each number. This is much more efficient than writing out separate instructions for each number, especially if you have a long list of numbers to add up.

Iteration and loop are closely related concepts, but they refer to slightly different things in the context of programming:

Loop: A loop is a control flow statement that allows code to be executed repeatedly. It is a structure in programming that repeats a block of code as long as a specified condition is true. There are different types of loops, including "for" loops, "while" loops, each with its own specific use case.

Iteration: Iteration is the act of repeating a process with the aim of approaching a desired goal or target. In programming, iteration usually refers to the single execution of the block of code within a loop. Every time the code inside the loop is executed, it is called an iteration.

For example, let's say we have a loop that runs five times and inside the loop, we print the current loop count. Here, the loop is the entire structure that allows us to repeat the print statement, while each individual print statement execution is an iteration.

In other words, a loop is the mechanism that facilitates repetition, while iteration is each individual repetition itself.

In this chapter, we will explore the loops, their syntax, and their applications in Python.

For Loop

The for loop is used to iterate over a sequence of items (such as a list, tuple, or string) or to repeat a block of code a specified number of times. It follows this general syntax:

```python
for item in sequence:
    # code to execute for each item
```

Here is an example that prints the elements of a list:

```python
fruits = ['apple', 'orange', 'banana']
for fruit in fruits:
    print(fruit)
```

You can also use the range() function to generate a sequence of numbers for iteration:

```python
for i in range(5):
    print(i)
```

This will print the numbers 0 to 4, as range() generates a sequence of numbers starting from 0 (by default) and ending one before the specified value.

While Loop

The while loop is used to repeatedly execute a block of code as long as a specified condition is true. It follows this general syntax:

```python
while condition:
    # code to execute while the condition is true
```

Here is an example that prints numbers from 1 to 5:

```python
number = 1
while number <= 5:
    print(number)
    number += 1
```

In this example, the loop will continue to execute as long as number is less than or equal to 5.

Loop Control Statements

Python provides several control statements that you can use to manage the flow of your loops:

- break: Immediately exits the current loop.
- continue: Skips the rest of the current iteration and continues with the next one.
- pass: A no-op statement that serves as a placeholder where code is required syntactically.

Example of using break:

```python
for i in range(5):
    if i == 3:
        break
    print(i)
```

This will print 0, 1, and 2, as the loop will terminate when i equals 3.

Nested Loops

You can use loops inside other loops, which is known as nesting. Here is an example of nested for loops:

```python
for i in range(3):
    for j in range(3):
        print(i, j)
```

This will print pairs of numbers (0,0), (0,1), (0,2), (1,0), and so on, as the inner loop iterates three times for each iteration of the outer loop.

List Comprehensions

List comprehensions are a concise way to create lists using a single line of code. They use a for loop and can include conditions. Here is an example:

```python
squares = [x**2 for x in range(5)]
```

This will create a list of squares of the numbers from 0 to 4.

Loops are essential for many tasks in programming, such as data processing, simulations, and algorithm implementations. They allow you to automate repetitive tasks, making your code more efficient and easier to read.

## CHAPTER 9

FUNCTIONS AND MODULES

Python functions and modules are essential concepts that every programmer should be familiar with. Functions allow us to break down our code into smaller, reusable pieces, while modules help us to organize our functions and variables into separate files for easier maintenance and readability.

Functions

What is a Function?

Imagine you have a blender in your kitchen. You use it to make smoothies. When you want to make a smoothie, you put some ingredients into the blender, like fruits and yogurt, and then you press a button to start it. After a few seconds, you get a tasty smoothie.

Now, let's think of the blender as a function. In this analogy:

- The ingredients you put into the blender are like the inputs (or arguments) of a function.
- The action of blending is what the function does to process the inputs.
- The smoothie you get at the end is the output (or return value) of the function.
-

So, in a computer program, a function works in a similar way. You give it some information, it processes that information by performing some actions, and then it gives you back some results. Just like using a blender to make different kinds of smoothies, you can use a function to perform different tasks in your program.

A function is a block of reusable code that performs a specific task. It takes inputs, called arguments or parameters, processes them, and returns an output. Functions in Python are defined using the def keyword.

Basic Function Syntax

```python
def function_name(parameters):
    # Function code
    return result  # Optional
```

For example, a simple function that adds two numbers together:

```python
def add(x, y):
    return x + y

result = add(5, 3)
print(result)  # Output: 8
```

Function Parameters and Arguments

When defining a function, we specify parameters that the function will take as input. When calling the function, we pass actual values, called arguments, to these parameters.

Variable-length Arguments

Sometimes, you may want to define a function that can accept any number of arguments. In Python, you can do this using the * and ** prefixes.

```python
def print_args(*args):
    for arg in args:
        print(arg)

print_args(1, 'hello', True, None)
```

Return Statement

Functions can return values to the caller using the return statement. Once the return statement is executed, the function exits, and control is passed back to the caller.

Local and Global Variables

Variables defined within a function are local to that function and can't be accessed outside the function. Conversely, variables defined outside a function are global and can be accessed and modified within a function.

A global variable is a variable that is declared outside of any function. Because it's not tied to any specific function, it can be accessed from any function in your code. Here's how to use a global variable inside a function in Python:

1. Declare a variable outside of any function, at the top-level of your script. This makes it a global variable.

python

```python
my_global_variable = 10
```

In the function where you want to use the global variable, you simply use its name. You don't have to declare it inside the function.

```python
def my_function():
    print(my_global_variable)
```

If you want to modify the global variable inside a function, you need to tell Python that you're referring to the global variable and not creating a new local variable. You do this using the global keyword.

```python
def my_function():
    global my_global_variable
    my_global_variable = 20
```

In this example, we first declare my_global_variable outside of any function and set it to 10. Inside my_function, we tell Python that we're referring to the global variable with global my_global_variable. We then modify its value to 20.

After calling my_function, the value of my_global_variable will be changed to 20 at the global level.

Keep in mind that using global variables can make your code more complex and harder to understand, so it's often better to pass variables as arguments to functions and return values from functions instead of using global variables.

Modules

What is a Module?

A module is a file containing Python code, which can define functions, classes, and variables, as well as runnable code. The code in the module can be imported and used in other modules or scripts.

Basic Module Syntax

To create a module, simply save your Python code in a file with the .py extension. For example, create a file named mymodule.py.

```python
# mymodule.py
def greet(name):
    print(f"Hello, {name}!")
```

Importing Modules

To use the functions and variables from a module in another module or script, you need to import it using the import statement.

```python
import mymodule

mymodule.greet('Alice')  # Output: Hello, Alice!
```

You can also import specific items from a module using the from ... import ... statement.

```python
from mymodule import greet
```

```python
greet('Bob')  # Output: Hello, Bob!
```

The __name__ Variable

When a Python file is run, a special variable called __name__ is defined. If the file is being run as the main program, __name__ is set to '__main__'. If the file is being imported as a module, __name__ is set to the module's name.

Standard Modules

Python comes with a wide variety of standard modules that you can use in your programs. These modules provide functions, classes, and types for various purposes, eliminating the need to write every piece of code from scratch. Here's an overview of some of the most useful standard modules in Python:

math - This module provides mathematical functions, including trigonometric, logarithmic, and other basic operations. It also contains constants like pi and e.

```python
import math
print(math.sqrt(16)) # Output: 4.0
```

random - This module provides functions for generating random numbers.

```python
import random
print(random.randint(1, 10))  # Output: a random number between 1 and 10
```

os - The os module provides functions for interacting with the operating system. It includes functions for file and directory management, process management, and more.

```python
import os
print(os.getcwd()) # Output: the current working directory
```

sys - This module provides access to variables and functions that interact with the Python runtime environment.

```python
import sys
print(sys.argv) # Output: list of command-line arguments passed to the script
```

datetime - This module provides classes for working with dates and times.

```python
from datetime import datetime
print(datetime.now()) # Output: the current date and time
```

json - This module provides functions for working with JSON data. You can encode Python objects into JSON format, and decode JSON data into Python objects.

```python
import json
data = {"name": "John", "age": 30}
json_string = json.dumps(data) # Output: '{"name": "John", "age": 30}'
```

re - This module provides functions for working with regular expressions.

```python
import re
pattern = re.compile(r'\d{3}-\d{2}-\d{4}')
match = pattern.search('SSN: 123-45-6789')
print(match.group()) # Output: '123-45-6789'
```

collections - This module provides additional data types beyond the built-in ones, like namedtuples, deque, Counter, and more.

```python
from collections import Counter
count = Counter(['a', 'b', 'c', 'a', 'b', 'b', 'c'])
print(count) # Output: Counter({'b': 3, 'a': 2, 'c': 2})
```

urllib - This module provides functions for working with URLs, including fetching data from the web.

```python
from urllib.request import urlopen
response = urlopen('https://www.example.com')
print(response.read()) # Output: the content of the webpage
```

pickle - This module provides functions for serializing (pickling) and deserializing (unpickling) Python objects.

```python
import pickle
data = {'foo': 'bar'}
with open('data.pkl', 'wb') as file:
    pickle.dump(data, file)
with open('data.pkl', 'rb') as file:
    loaded_data = pickle.load(file)
print(loaded_data) # Output: {'foo': 'bar'}
```

These are just a few of the many standard modules available in Python. Each module is designed for a specific purpose and can significantly reduce the time it takes to develop and test your programs.

## CHAPTER 10

HANDLING EXCEPTIONS AND ERRORS

Error handling is crucial in any programming language, including Python. Proper error handling ensures that your program can run smoothly, even when unexpected situations occur. Here are some of the primary reasons why error handling is so important:

Enhanced Robustness: Error handling allows a program to continue executing even when an error occurs, preventing it from crashing unexpectedly. This makes your program more stable and robust, as it can handle different situations gracefully.

Improved User Experience: When errors occur, your program can provide informative error messages, making it easier for users to understand what went wrong. This leads to a better user experience, as users can take appropriate action instead of being left in the dark.

Easier Debugging: By handling errors and providing detailed error messages, you can more easily identify and fix issues in your code. This makes the debugging process much more efficient and helps you maintain a higher quality codebase.

Better Resource Management: Some errors may arise from resource issues, such as trying to open a file that does not exist or running out of memory. Proper error handling can help you manage resources more effectively, ensuring that your program can recover from such situations.

Increased Security: Proper error handling can also prevent security vulnerabilities. For example, if an attacker tries to exploit your program, well-handled errors can prevent them from gaining unauthorized access or causing damage.

Compliance with Best Practices: Proper error handling is considered a best practice in software development. Following best practices makes your code more readable, maintainable, and easier for others to understand.

When programming, errors are a natural part of the process. However, they can disrupt the flow of your program and cause it to crash unexpectedly. To deal with this, Python provides a way to handle errors gracefully through exceptions and error handling.

Types of Errors

Syntax errors and exceptions are both types of errors that can occur in Python code. However, they occur at different stages of the program's execution and are caused by different types of issues. Let's take a closer look at both.

Syntax Errors

These are errors that occur when the Python parser encounters code that doesn't follow the rules of the Python language. These errors are detected before the program starts running, during the parsing phase. Syntax errors are often called "parsing errors" for this reason. Common examples of syntax errors include:
- Misspelled keywords (e.g., "whiel" instead of "while")

- Incorrectly matched parentheses or brackets (e.g., "print(1 + 2]" instead of "print(1 + 2)")
- Missing colons in control statements (e.g., "if x > 5" instead of "if x > 5:")
- Incorrect indentation (e.g., inconsistent use of tabs and spaces)

Syntax errors prevent the program from running at all. When Python encounters a syntax error, it displays an error message with the filename, line number, and an indication of where the error occurred.

Exceptions

These are errors that occur during the execution of a program. Exceptions are raised when the program encounters a situation that it cannot handle or when an operation results in an error. Python has built-in exceptions for various types of errors, such as division by zero, attempting to access an element that doesn't exist in a list, or trying to open a file that doesn't exist. Examples of exceptions include:
- ZeroDivisionError: Raised when attempting to divide by zero
- FileNotFoundError: Raised when trying to open a file that doesn't exist
- KeyError: Raised when attempting to access a dictionary key that doesn't exist
- TypeError: Raised when an operation is performed on an object of the wrong type

Exceptions can be caught and handled using try-except blocks. When an exception is raised, the program's execution is interrupted, and Python looks for an appropriate except block to handle the exception. If no suitable except block is found, the program terminates and displays an error message.

Basic Exception Handling

To handle exceptions, Python provides the try, except statement. The basic structure is:

python
```python
try:
    # code that may cause an error
except ExceptionType:
    # code to handle the error
```

For example:

python
```python
try:
    result = 10 / 0
except ZeroDivisionError:
    print("Cannot divide by zero!")
```

In this example, the code within the try block will attempt to divide by zero, which will raise a ZeroDivisionError. The code in the except block will then run, printing "Cannot divide by zero!" to the console.

Multiple Exceptions

You can catch multiple exceptions by specifying multiple except blocks:

python
```python
try:
    # code that may cause an error
except (ExceptionType1, ExceptionType2):
    # code to handle ExceptionType1 or ExceptionType2
except ExceptionType3:
    # code to handle ExceptionType3
```

The else Clause

You can use the else clause after all the except clauses. The code inside the else block will run if the try block does not raise any exceptions:

```python
try:
    # code that may cause an error
except ExceptionType:
    # code to handle the error
else:
    # code to run if no error occurred
```

The finally Clause

The finally clause is used to define clean-up actions that must be executed under all circumstances. It runs regardless of whether an exception occurred or not:

```python
try:
    # code that may cause an error
except ExceptionType:
    # code to handle the error
finally:
    # code to run no matter what
```

Raising Exceptions

You can also raise exceptions in your code using the raise statement:

```python
if x < 0:
    raise ValueError("x cannot be negative")
```

In this example, a ValueError will be raised if x is less than 0.

Creating Custom Exceptions

Python allows you to create your own exceptions by creating a new exception class derived from the Exception base class:

```python
class MyCustomError(Exception):
    pass
```

You can then raise your custom exception using the raise statement:

```python
raise MyCustomError("This is a custom error message")
```

Below is an example of a Python script that tries to open a file, read the contents, and then convert it to an integer. However, the code contains a few potential points of failure that might cause exceptions.

```python
import traceback

def read_and_convert(filename):
    try:
        with open(filename, 'r') as f:
            content = f.read()
            number = int(content)
            return number
    except Exception as e:
        print("An exception occurred!")
        print("Exception Type:", type(e).__name__)
        print("Exception Message:", str(e))
        print("Stack Trace:")
```

```
        traceback.print_exc()

filename = "example.txt"
result = read_and_convert(filename)
print("Result:", result)
```

In this example, the code is wrapped in a try block. If an exception occurs, the code inside the except block will run. It will print the type of the exception, the message of the exception, and the stack trace. The stack trace is particularly useful for understanding the context and flow of execution that led to the exception. The traceback module is used to print the stack trace.

You can test this code by creating a file named example.txt and putting some text inside it. Try different contents, such as a valid integer, a non-integer string, or leave the file empty, and see how the code handles different exceptions.

Troubleshooting The Exceptions

Understanding what happened in an exception involves a combination of analyzing the exception message, the stack trace, and the context in which the exception occurred.

Read the Exception Message: The exception message usually gives a direct explanation of what went wrong. For example, a ZeroDivisionError with the message "division by zero" tells you that the code tried to divide a number by zero, which is not allowed.

Analyze the Stack Trace: When an exception occurs, Python provides a stack trace that shows the sequence of function calls that led to the exception. The stack trace provides information about where the exception occurred and what the program was doing at the time. It shows the lines of code involved in each function call, starting from the most recent call and working its way back to the original call. By following the stack trace, you can find the exact line of code where the exception was raised and understand the flow of execution that led to the error.

Review the Code Context: Go to the line of code where the exception occurred, as indicated by the stack trace, and review the surrounding code. Consider the values of variables, the logic of the code, and the expected behavior of any functions or methods being called. Pay attention to any conditions or loops that might be relevant to the exception.

Reproduce the Error: If you can, try to reproduce the error by running the code with the same inputs or under the same conditions that led to the exception. This will help you observe the behavior of the code and confirm your understanding of the issue.

Use Debugging Tools: Tools like Python's built-in pdb module or interactive debugging tools in Integrated Development Environments (IDEs) like PyCharm, Visual Studio Code, or Eclipse can be helpful. You can set breakpoints, step through the code, inspect variable values, and evaluate expressions to gain a deeper understanding of the code's behavior and the cause of the exception.

Consult Documentation and Resources: If the exception is related to a specific library or module, consult its documentation to understand the expected behavior and any potential pitfalls. Online resources like Stack Overflow can also be helpful, as others may have encountered similar exceptions and shared their solutions.

Remember, exceptions are a natural part of programming, and understanding them is a skill that develops with experience. Take the time to analyze exceptions thoroughly, test your assumptions, and learn from each occurrence.

## CHAPTER 11

FILE I/O AND DATA STORAGE

File Input/Output (I/O) operations in Python are critical for a wide range of applications, from simple scripts to complex data analysis tools. Python's built-in functions for file handling make it easy to read from and write to files, enabling programmers to interact with data stored on the disk. This is essential for long-term data storage, sharing data across different applications, and processing large data sets that don't fit into memory.

In Python, the open function is used to open a file for reading, writing, or appending. Python supports a variety of file formats, including plain text files, CSV files, and binary files. Once a file is opened, Python provides a series of methods for reading data from or writing data to the file. For example, the read method can read the entire contents of a file, while the write method can write data to a file.

File I/O in Python is particularly useful for data storage and data analysis tasks. Data scientists and analysts often work with large data sets stored in CSV or Excel files. Python's file I/O capabilities, combined with popular libraries like pandas and numpy, make it easy to read, process and analyze these data sets.

File I/O is also essential for configuration files, logs, and other types of files used in software development. Configuration files allow developers to customize the behavior of an application without changing its code. Log files record events, errors, and other information about an application's execution, helping developers diagnose and fix problems.

Opening Files

In Python, we use the open function to open a file. The open function takes two arguments: the file name and the mode in which the file should be opened.

python
```python
file = open("example.txt", "r") # Opens the file in read mode
```

The most commonly used file modes are:
- 'r': read mode
- 'w': write mode
- 'a': append mode
- 'b': binary mode

Reading from Files

Once the file is opened in read mode ('r'), we can use the read method to read the entire file or the readline method to read a single line.

python
```python
file = open("example.txt", "r")
content = file.read()
print(content)
file.close()
```

Writing to Files

To write data to a file, open the file in write mode ('w') or append mode ('a'). Then use the write method to write data to the file.

```python
file = open("example.txt", "w")
file.write("Hello, Python!")
file.close()
```

Closing Files

After performing the required file operations, it is essential to close the file using the close method. Closing the file frees up system resources.

```python
file.close()
```

Using with Statements

An alternative to manually closing files is to use the with statement. It ensures that the file is automatically closed when the block of code is exited.

```python
with open("example.txt", "r") as file:
    content = file.read()
    print(content)
```

Working with JSON

JSON (JavaScript Object Notation) is a lightweight data-interchange format widely used for data storage and exchange. Python has a built-in module called json that allows you to work with JSON data.

```python
import json
```

```python
data = {
    "name": "John",
    "age": 30,
    "city": "New York"
}

with open("data.json", "w") as file:
    json.dump(data, file)

with open("data.json", "r") as file:
    loaded_data = json.load(file)
    print(loaded_data)
```

Pickling

Python provides the pickle module to serialize (convert to bytes) and deserialize (convert back to the original format) Python objects. This is useful for saving complex objects to files.

```python
import pickle

data = {"name": "John", "age": 30, "city": "New York"}

with open("data.pkl", "wb") as file:
    pickle.dump(data, file)

with open("data.pkl", "rb") as file:
    loaded_data = pickle.load(file)
    print(loaded_data)
```

SQLite

SQLite is a C library that provides a lightweight, disk-based database that doesn't require a separate server process.

Python has a built-in module called sqlite3 to work with SQLite databases.

```python
import sqlite3

conn = sqlite3.connect("example.db") # Creates or opens a database file
cursor = conn.cursor()

cursor.execute('''CREATE TABLE IF NOT EXISTS users (id INTEGER PRIMARY KEY, name TEXT, age INTEGER)''')

cursor.execute("INSERT INTO users (name, age) VALUES (?, ?)", ("John", 30))

conn.commit()

cursor.execute("SELECT * FROM users")
print(cursor.fetchall())

conn.close()
```

Managing file paths and directories in Python is made easier by the os and os.path modules. These modules provide a range of functions to handle file paths, directories, and file system operations, allowing you to interact with the file system in a platform-independent manner.
Here are some common tasks you might need to perform and how to do them in Python:

Creating Directories: Use the os.mkdir function to create a new directory. If you need to create multiple nested directories, you can use the os.makedirs function.

```python
import os

# Create a single directory
os.mkdir("example_dir")

# Create multiple nested directories
os.makedirs("example_dir/sub_dir1/sub_dir2")
```

Listing Files and Directories: The os.listdir function returns a list of all files and directories in a given directory.

```python
import os

contents = os.listdir("example_dir")
print(contents)  # Output: ['file1.txt', 'file2.txt', 'sub_dir1']
```

Changing the Current Working Directory: Use the os.chdir function to change the current working directory to a specified path.

```python
import os

os.chdir("example_dir")
print(os.getcwd())  # Output: '/full/path/to/example_dir'
```

Checking if a Path Exists: The os.path.exists function can be used to check if a path exists.

```python
import os

print(os.path.exists("example_dir"))  # Output: True
print(os.path.exists("nonexistent_dir"))  # Output: False
```

Getting the Absolute Path: The os.path.abspath function returns the absolute path of a given path.

python
```python
import os

absolute_path = os.path.abspath("example_dir")
print(absolute_path)  # Output: '/full/path/to/example_dir'
```

Joining Paths: Use the os.path.join function to join multiple paths. This function handles platform-specific differences in path separators.

python
```python
import os

path = os.path.join("example_dir", "sub_dir1", "file1.txt")
print(path)    # Output: 'example_dir/sub_dir1/file1.txt' (Linux/OSX)
```

Splitting Paths: The os.path.split function splits a path into a directory and a file. The os.path.splitext function splits a filename into a name and an extension.

python
```python
import os

dir, file = os.path.split("/path/to/file.txt")
print(dir)  # Output: '/path/to'
print(file)  # Output: 'file.txt'

name, ext = os.path.splitext("file.txt")
print(name)  # Output: 'file'
print(ext)  # Output: '.txt'
```

Deleting Files and Directories: Use the os.remove function to delete a file and the os.rmdir function to remove an empty directory. If you need to delete a directory and all its contents, you can use the shutil.rmtree function from the shutil module.

python
```python
import os
import shutil
# Delete a file
os.remove("example_dir/file1.txt")
# Delete an empty directory
os.rmdir("example_dir/empty_dir")
# Delete a directory and all its contents
shutil.rmtree("example_dir/sub_dir1")
```

These functions provide a foundation for managing file paths and directories in Python. By combining these functions, you can perform complex file system operations and automate tasks like file organization, data analysis, and more.

## CHAPTER 12

DICTIONARIES AND DATA STRUCTURES

In Python, data structures are used to store and organize data in a way that enables efficient access and modification. Among the different types of data structures available in Python, dictionaries are one of the most versatile and powerful.

Dictionaries

A dictionary is an unordered collection of data stored as key-value pairs. Each key is unique and associated with a single value. Dictionaries are defined using curly braces {}, and the key-value pairs are separated by commas.

One of the key advantages of dictionaries is that they allow for efficient data retrieval. When you know the key, you can retrieve the corresponding value in constant time, regardless of the size of the dictionary. This is because dictionaries are implemented as hash tables.

Dictionaries store data in key-value pairs, which makes them highly suitable for situations where data is naturally represented as pairs of associated values.

Dictionaries can store values of different data types, including other dictionaries, making them very versatile. Moreover, the keys can be of any hashable data type. Since dictionary keys must be unique, dictionaries automatically handle duplicates by overwriting the old value with the new value for a given key. This can be useful when you want to avoid duplicate entries.

Dictionaries are inherently unordered, meaning the order of key-value pairs may differ from when they were added. While Python 3.7+ maintains insertion order as an implementation detail, it is not guaranteed in earlier versions or other programming languages. Due to their internal hash table implementation, dictionaries tend to consume more memory than other data structures like lists or tuples. This can be an issue when working with a large amount of data.

The keys in a dictionary must be hashable and, therefore, immutable, which limits the types of data that can be used as keys. For example, you cannot use lists or other dictionaries as keys. Dictionaries do not support the inherent sorting of keys or values. If you need sorted data, you will have to use additional operations or data structures.

Creating Dictionaries

To create a dictionary, you can use the curly braces syntax and specify the key-value pairs separated by a colon:

```python
student = {
    "name": "John",
    "age": 25,
    "major": "Computer Science"
}
```

Alternatively, you can use the dict constructor:

```python
student = dict(name="John", age=25, major="Computer
Science")
```

Accessing Values

To access a value from a dictionary, you use the corresponding
key inside square brackets:

```python
name = student["name"]  # "John"
```

If you try to access a key that doesn't exist, a KeyError will be
raised. To avoid this, you can use the get method:

```python
name = student.get("name", "Unknown")  # "John"
gender = student.get("gender", "Unknown")  # "Unknown"
```

Modifying and Adding Values

You can modify the value associated with a key by assigning a
new value to it:

```python
student["age"] = 26
```

To add a new key-value pair, you simply assign a value to a
new key:

```python
student["gender"] = "Male"
```

Removing Values

You can remove a key-value pair using the del statement:

```python
del student["major"]
```

To remove a key-value pair and get the value at the same time, you can use the pop method:

```python
major = student.pop("major", None)
```

Iterating Through Dictionaries

You can iterate through the keys, values, or both using the keys, values, and items methods, respectively:

```python
for key in student.keys():
    print(key)
for value in student.values():
    print(value)
for key, value in student.items():
    print(key, value)
```

Other Data Structures

Besides dictionaries, Python offers other data structures, each with its own characteristics and use cases:

Tuples

Tuples are similar to lists in Python, but they are immutable, meaning once a tuple is created, it cannot be modified. This immutability makes tuples slightly faster than lists when it comes to iteration. Tuples are typically used for data that should not be changed, such as days of the week or dates on a calendar.

Here's the basic syntax for creating a tuple:

```python
my_tuple = (item1, item2, item3, ...)
```

Here's a simple example of creating a tuple:

```python
weekdays = ("Monday", "Tuesday", "Wednesday", "Thursday", "Friday", "Saturday", "Sunday")
print(weekdays)
```

You can access elements of a tuple by index, just like you would with a list:

```python
# Accessing the first element
print(weekdays[0])  # Output: 'Monday'

# Accessing the last element
print(weekdays[-1])  # Output: 'Sunday'

# Slicing a tuple (get elements from 1 to 3)
print(weekdays[1:4])    # Output: ('Tuesday', 'Wednesday', 'Thursday')
```

Tuples can also be used to assign multiple variables at once:

```python
(a, b, c) = (1, 2, 3)
print(a)  # Output: 1
print(b)  # Output: 2
print(c)  # Output: 3
```

Tuples are often used for functions that return multiple values:

python
```python
def get_name_and_age():
    return ("Alice", 30)
(name, age) = get_name_and_age()
print(name)  # Output: 'Alice'
print(age)   # Output: 30
```

You can also use tuples to create a list of pairs or other combinations:

python
```python
students = [("John", 25), ("Anna", 22), ("Mike", 20)]
```

In this example, each element of the students list is a tuple containing a name and an age.

Sets

A set is an unordered collection of unique elements. It's like a list, but it can't have duplicates. Sets are often used to eliminate duplicate values from a list or to test membership of an element.

Here's a simple example of creating and using a set:

python
```python
# Creating a set
my_set = {1, 2, 3, 4, 5}
print(my_set) # Output: {1, 2, 3, 4, 5}
# Adding an element to a set
my_set.add(6)
print(my_set)  # Output: {1, 2, 3, 4, 5, 6}

# Removing an element from a set
my_set.remove(6)
```

```python
print(my_set)  # Output: {1, 2, 3, 4, 5}

# Using a set to remove duplicates from a list
my_list = [1, 2, 2, 3, 4, 4, 5]
unique_list = list(set(my_list))
print(unique_list)  # Output: [1, 2, 3, 4, 5]
```

Stacks

A stack is a last-in, first-out (LIFO) data structure. It's like a stack of plates; you can only add or remove plates from the top of the stack. Stacks are commonly used in algorithms that require a depth-first search.

Here's an example of implementing a stack using a list:

```python
# Creating a stack
my_stack = []

# Pushing (adding) an element onto the stack
my_stack.append(1)
my_stack.append(2)
my_stack.append(3)
print(my_stack)  # Output: [1, 2, 3]

# Popping (removing) an element off the stack
top_element = my_stack.pop()
print(top_element)  # Output: 3
print(my_stack)  # Output: [1, 2]
```

Queues

A queue is a first-in, first-out (FIFO) data structure. It's like a line of people waiting for a bus; the person who arrives first gets on the bus first. Queues are commonly used in algorithms that require a breadth-first search.

Here's an example of implementing a queue using a list:

python
```python
# Creating a queue
my_queue = []

# Enqueue (adding) an element to the queue
my_queue.append(1)
my_queue.append(2)
my_queue.append(3)
print(my_queue)  # Output: [1, 2, 3]

# Dequeue (removing) an element from the queue
first_element = my_queue.pop(0)
print(first_element)  # Output: 1
print(my_queue)  # Output: [2, 3]
```

Note: Lists in Python are not the most efficient way to implement queues. A better way is to use the collections.deque class.

python
```python
from collections import deque

# Creating a queue
my_queue = deque()

# Enqueue (adding) an element to the queue
my_queue.append(1)
my_queue.append(2)
my_queue.append(3)
print(my_queue)  # Output: deque([1, 2, 3])
```

```python
# Dequeue (removing) an element from the queue
first_element = my_queue.popleft()
print(first_element)  # Output: 1
print(my_queue)  # Output: deque([2, 3])
```

Next we will learn about Object-Oriented Programming!

## CHAPTER 13

OBJECT-ORIENTED PROGRAMMING (OOP)

Object-Oriented Programming (OOP) is a paradigm that allows you to design and structure your code based on real-world entities and their relationships. In OOP, we organize code into "objects," which represent entities, and "classes," which define the blueprint for objects. Objects can have attributes (data) and methods (functions) associated with them.
Python, being a versatile language, fully supports OOP and allows you to create powerful and reusable code structures.

Classes

A class is a blueprint for creating objects. It is a user-defined prototype for an object that defines a set of attributes that characterize any object of the class. The attributes are data members (class variables and instance variables) and methods, accessed via dot notation. A class is a way of grouping functions and variables under a single name, so they can be used more easily and efficiently. In Python, classes are defined using the class keyword.

For example:

```python
class Car:
    pass
```

Here, Car is the name of the class.

Objects

An object is an instance of a class. It is a basic unit of OOP and represents the real-life entities. An object encompasses both data members (class variables, instance variables) and methods. The process of creating an object from a class is called instantiation. In Python, you can create an object by calling the class:

python
```python
my_car = Car()
```

Here, my_car is an object (or instance) of the class Car.

When an object is created from a class, it inherits all the attributes and methods defined in the class. Each object can also have its own attributes that are unique to that instance.

Therefore, a class is a blueprint for creating objects, and an object is an instance of a class with specific attributes and methods. Classes define the general structure and behavior of an object, while objects represent specific instances with particular data.

Attributes and Methods

Attributes are variables that store data for an object, while methods are functions that define the behavior of the object. In our Car class, let's define some attributes and methods:

python
```python
class Car:
```

```python
    def __init__(self, brand, model, color):
        self.brand = brand
        self.model = model
        self.color = color
        self.speed = 0

    def accelerate(self):
        self.speed += 10
        return self.speed

    def brake(self):
        self.speed -= 10
        return self.speed

    def honk(self):
        return "Honk! Honk!"
```

Here, the __init__ method is a special method called a constructor. It gets executed when an object is created. The self parameter is a reference to the object itself.

Now, let's create an object and use its methods:

```python
my_car = Car("Toyota", "Corolla", "Red")
print(my_car.brand) # Output: Toyota
print(my_car.accelerate()) # Output: 10
print(my_car.brake()) # Output: 0
print(my_car.honk()) # Output: Honk! Honk!
```

Inheritance

Inheritance is a fundamental concept in object-oriented programming (OOP) that allows a class (called a subclass or child class) to inherit attributes and methods from another class (called a superclass or parent class). It is a way to create a new class that is a modified version of an existing class. The new class retains the characteristics of the existing class and can have additional attributes and methods or override the inherited ones. Inheritance represents a relationship between two classes, where one class is a more specific version of another.

Inheritance allows you to define a class that inherits all the methods and properties from another class. The class that inherits is called the **derived** or **child** class, and the class being inherited from is the **base** or **parent** class.

For example, let's create a SportsCar class that inherits from the Car class:

```python
class SportsCar(Car):
    def __init__(self, brand, model, color):
        super().__init__(brand, model, color)
        self.spoiler = True

    def accelerate(self):
        self.speed += 20
        return self.speed
```

Here, the super() function allows us to call the constructor of the parent class.

Now, let's create an object of the SportsCar class:

```python
my_sports_car = SportsCar("Ferrari", "488", "Yellow")
print(my_sports_car.accelerate()) # Output: 20
```

One of the main advantages of inheritance is code reusability. You can define common attributes and methods in a base class and inherit them in derived classes without rewriting the code. It allows you to extend the functionality of existing classes. You can add new attributes and methods or modify the inherited ones in the derived classes to cater to specific needs.

Inheritance helps in establishing a logical structure for your classes. You can create a hierarchical relationship between classes, which represents the "is-a" relationship and makes it easier to understand the relationships between classes. It also enables polymorphism, a powerful OOP concept that allows objects of different classes to be treated as objects of a common parent class. It makes the code more flexible and easier to maintain.

Inheritance helps in encapsulating the common attributes and methods in a single parent class, keeping the code organized and making it easier to manage and maintain.

Polymorphism

Polymorphism is a fundamental concept in object-oriented programming (OOP) that allows objects of different classes to be treated as objects of a common superclass. The word "polymorphism" comes from the Greek words "poly" meaning "many" and "morph" meaning "form", so polymorphism literally means "many forms". In the context of OOP, polymorphism refers to the ability of a single function or method to work with different types of objects.

There are two main types of polymorphism: compile-time polymorphism and runtime polymorphism.

Compile-time Polymorphism (Method Overloading): This type of polymorphism occurs when multiple methods with the same name but different parameters are defined in a class. The method called is determined at compile-time based on the method signature (number and type of parameters). This is also known as method overloading.

Runtime Polymorphism (Method Overriding): This type of polymorphism occurs when a subclass provides a specific implementation of a method that is already defined in its superclass. The method called is determined at runtime based on the object's class. This is also known as method overriding.

For example, we can create a function that takes a car object and accelerates it:

```python
def race(car):
    return car.accelerate()

print(race(my_car)) # Output: 10
print(race(my_sports_car)) # Output: 40
```

Even though my_car and my_sports_car are instances of different classes, they can be passed to the race function because they share the same base class and method.

Here is another example of runtime polymorphism in Python:

```python
class Animal:
    def speak(self):
        pass

class Dog(Animal):
    def speak(self):
```

```python
        return "Woof!"

class Cat(Animal):
    def speak(self):
        return "Meow!"

# Polymorphism
def animal_sound(animal):
    return animal.speak()

dog = Dog()
cat = Cat()

print(animal_sound(dog)) # Output: Woof!
print(animal_sound(cat)) # Output: Meow!
```

In the example above, the animal_sound function accepts an object of type Animal (or any subclass of Animal) and calls the speak method on it. Depending on the actual class of the object passed (either Dog or Cat), the corresponding speak method is called at runtime.

Polymorphism provides flexibility and makes it easier to extend and maintain code. It allows you to write more general code that works with objects of different classes, as long as they share a common interface (i.e., they have the same methods). This promotes code reusability and makes the code more modular and readable.

Encapsulation

Encapsulation is one of the four fundamental principles of object-oriented programming (OOP), the other three being inheritance, polymorphism, and abstraction. Encapsulation refers to the practice of hiding the details of an object's internal state and requiring that interaction with the object be performed through well-defined interfaces.

In other words, encapsulation is all about creating a "black box" or a "shell" around an object that shields the object's internal workings from the outside world. This is done by restricting access to certain parts of an object while exposing a few select attributes and methods that are deemed safe for public use.

Here's how encapsulation can be implemented in Python:

Private Attributes and Methods: In Python, you can make an attribute or method private by prefixing its name with a double underscore (e.g., __private_attribute). This will "mangle" the name of the attribute or method, making it less accessible from outside the class. It's not truly private, as it can still be accessed by determined programmers, but it's a strong hint that it should not be touched from outside the class.

Public Attributes and Methods: These are the parts of an object that are meant to be accessed from outside the class. They make up the object's public interface.

Getters and Setters: These are special methods that allow you to control the access and modification of private attributes. A getter is used to read the value of a private attribute, while a setter is used to modify it.

Here's an example in Python that demonstrates encapsulation:

```python
class Person:
    def __init__(self, name, age):
        self.__name = name # private attribute
        self.__age = age   # private attribute
```

```python
        # getter for name
        def get_name(self):
            return self.__name

        # setter for name
        def set_name(self, name):
            self.__name = name

        # getter for age
        def get_age(self):
            return self.__age

        # setter for age
        def set_age(self, age):
            if age > 0:
                self.__age = age
            else:
                print("Age must be a positive number")

# Usage
person = Person("John", 25)
print(person.get_name()) # Output: John
print(person.get_age())  # Output: 25
person.set_age(-5)           # Output: Age must be a positive
number
print(person.get_age())  # Output: 25
```

Encapsulation provides several benefits, including:

Control: It allows you to control how an object's attributes are accessed and modified.

Flexibility: You can change the internal implementation of an object without affecting the code that uses the object.

Security: It prevents unauthorized access and modification of an object's internal state.

Object-Oriented Programming in Python allows us to create robust, reusable, and organized code structures. By using classes, objects, inheritance, polymorphism, and encapsulation, we can design and implement complex systems that are easy to understand, maintain, and extend.

## CHAPTER 14

SIMPLE PROJECTS AND APPLICATIONS

In this chapter, we will explore some simple projects and applications that you can build using Python. These projects will help you practice your Python skills and learn more about the various tools and libraries available in Python. Let's dive right in.

Project 1: Calculator

A calculator application is a simple yet effective project to test your Python skills. You can create a basic calculator that can perform arithmetic operations such as addition, subtraction, multiplication, division, and even more advanced calculations like square roots, exponentiation, and more.

Tools Needed:

- Python's built-in functions and libraries

Steps to create the Calculator:

1. Create a user interface that allows users to select the type of operation they want to perform.
2. Create functions for each arithmetic operation.
3. Take user inputs for numbers.
4. Display the result after performing the chosen operation.

```python
def add(x, y):
    return x + y


def subtract(x, y):
```

```python
    return x - y

def multiply(x, y):
    return x * y

def divide(x, y):
    if y == 0:
        return "Cannot divide by zero!"
    return x / y

def exponent(x, y):
    return x ** y

def square_root(x):
    if x < 0:
        return "Cannot compute the square root of a negative
number!"
    return x ** 0.5

while True:
    print("Select operation:")
    print("1. Add")
    print("2. Subtract")
    print("3. Multiply")
    print("4. Divide")
    print("5. Exponent")
    print("6. Square Root")
    print("7. Exit")

    choice = input("Enter choice (1/2/3/4/5/6/7): ")

    if choice == '7':
        print("Exiting Calculator. Goodbye!")
        break
```

```python
if choice in ('1', '2', '3', '4', '5'):
    num1 = float(input("Enter first number: "))
    num2 = float(input("Enter second number: "))

if choice == '1':
    print(num1, "+", num2, "=", add(num1, num2))

elif choice == '2':
    print(num1, "-", num2, "=", subtract(num1, num2))

elif choice == '3':
    print(num1, "*", num2, "=", multiply(num1, num2))

elif choice == '4':
    result = divide(num1, num2)
    print(num1, "/", num2, "=", result)

elif choice == '5':
    print(num1, "^", num2, "=", exponent(num1, num2))

elif choice == '6':
    num = float(input("Enter the number: "))
    print("Square root of", num, "=", square_root(num))

else:
    print("Invalid Input")
```

This program presents a simple menu to the user where they can select an operation to perform. The program then reads the numbers from the user and performs the specified operation. It will keep presenting the menu to the user until they choose to exit by entering '7'. Note that this calculator does not handle complex numbers, and division by zero is checked for and handled.

Project 2: To-do List

A to-do list is a simple and practical project that can help you learn how to work with data in Python.

Tools Needed:
* Python's built-in functions and libraries

Steps to create the To-do List:
1. Create a list to store to-do items.
2. Create a user interface that allows users to add, remove, or view to-do items.
3. Implement functions to add items, remove items, and display the current to-do list.
4. You can further enhance the to-do list by allowing users to mark items as done, setting task deadlines, or sorting tasks based on priority.

Here's a simple Python program that acts as a command-line-based to-do list application. This program allows you to add tasks, remove tasks, and view the current list of tasks.

```python
tasks = []

def display_menu():
    print("\nToDo List:")
    print("1. Add Task")
    print("2. Remove Task")
    print("3. View Tasks")
    print("4. Exit")
```

```python
def add_task():
    task = input("Enter the task: ")
    tasks.append(task)
    print(f"Task '{task}' added successfully.")

def remove_task():
    task = input("Enter the task to remove: ")
    if task in tasks:
        tasks.remove(task)
        print(f"Task '{task}' removed successfully.")
    else:
        print(f"Task '{task}' not found.")

def view_tasks():
    if len(tasks) == 0:
        print("No tasks in the list.")
    else:
        print("\nTasks:")
        for i, task in enumerate(tasks):
            print(f"{i+1}. {task}")

def main():
    while True:
        display_menu()
        choice = input("Enter your choice: ")
        if choice == '1':
            add_task()
        elif choice == '2':
            remove_task()
        elif choice == '3':
            view_tasks()
        elif choice == '4':
            print("Exiting ToDo List. Goodbye!")
            break
        else:
```

```python
        print("Invalid choice. Please try again.")

if __name__ == "__main__":
    main()
```

This code displays a menu to the user where they can choose to add a task, remove a task, view the current tasks, or exit the program. It uses a simple list to store the tasks. Each time the user selects an option, the corresponding function is called to handle the request. This program runs in an infinite loop, presenting the menu to the user after every action until they choose to exit by entering '4'.

Project 3: Alarm Clock

An alarm clock is a useful application that can help you learn about Python's time-related functions and libraries.

Tools Needed:
- Python's built-in libraries like time and datetime

Steps to create the Alarm Clock:
1. Create a user interface that allows users to set the alarm time.
2. Use Python's time or datetime library to track the current time.
3. Compare the current time with the set alarm time.
4. Display an alert or play a sound when the current time matches the set alarm time.

Here's a simple Python code for an alarm clock that uses the datetime and time modules to set and trigger an alarm. This code lets you set an alarm by entering the time you want it to go off.

```python
import datetime
import time

def alarm():
    print("Set the time for the alarm in HH:MM format (24-hour format).")
    alarm_time = input("Alarm Time: ")
    alarm_hour, alarm_minute = map(int, alarm_time.split(':'))

    while True:
        now = datetime.datetime.now()
        current_hour = now.hour
        current_minute = now.minute

        if alarm_hour == current_hour and alarm_minute == current_minute:
            print("Alarm is ringing!")
            break
        else:
            time.sleep(1)

alarm()
```

In this example, the alarm function prompts you to enter the time for the alarm in HH:MM format (24-hour format). It then extracts the hour and minute values from the input string. The function continuously checks the current time, and when the current time matches the alarm time, it prints a message to indicate that the alarm is ringing. The function uses the time.sleep(1) statement to pause the execution for one second before checking the time again.

Please note that this example simply prints a message to the console when the alarm goes off. You could also add additional functionality to play a sound, send a notification, or trigger other actions when the alarm goes off.

Project 3: Text Based Game

Creating a text-based game in Python is a great way to practice your programming skills while creating something fun and interactive. A simple text-based game could be a "choose your own adventure" style game, where the player makes choices that lead to different outcomes.

Tools Needed:
- Python's built-in functions and libraries

Steps to create the Text-based game:

1. Create a "choose your own adventure" style game
2. The player makes choices that lead to different outcomes.

Here is a simple example of a text-based adventure game in Python:

```python
def main():
    print("You wake up in a dark room. You have two choices:")
    print("1. Turn on the light.")
    print("2. Stay in the dark.")
    choice = input("What do you choose? ")

    if choice == "1":
        print("You turn on the light and find yourself in a small room.")
        light_room()
    elif choice == "2":
```

```python
            print("You stay in the dark and eventually fall back
asleep.")
        dark_room()
    else:
        print("Invalid choice. Please try again.")
        main()

def light_room():
    print("You are in a small room with a door.")
    print("1. Open the door.")
    print("2. Stay in the room.")
    choice = input("What do you choose? ")

    if choice == "1":
        print("You open the door and find a staircase.")
        staircase()
    elif choice == "2":
            print("You stay in the room and eventually fall back
asleep.")
        dark_room()
    else:
        print("Invalid choice. Please try again.")
        light_room()

def dark_room():
    print("You are in a dark room.")
    print("You hear something moving.")
    print("1. Turn on the light.")
    print("2. Stay in the dark.")
    choice = input("What do you choose? ")

    if choice == "1":
            print("You turn on the light and find yourself in a small
room.")
        light_room()
```

```python
    elif choice == "2":
            print("You stay in the dark and eventually fall back
asleep.")
        main()
    else:
        print("Invalid choice. Please try again.")
        dark_room()

def staircase():
    print("You are at the top of a staircase.")
    print("1. Go down the stairs.")
    print("2. Go back to the room.")
    choice = input("What do you choose? ")

    if choice == "1":
        print("You go down the stairs and find yourself outside.")
        print("Congratulations! You've escaped the room.")
    elif choice == "2":
        print("You go back to the room and eventually fall back
asleep.")
        dark_room()
    else:
        print("Invalid choice. Please try again.")
        staircase()

main()
```

In this example, the player wakes up in a dark room and has to make choices to find a way out. The game consists of several functions representing different rooms or situations. Each function provides the player with choices that lead to different outcomes and move the player through the game. The game continues until the player successfully escapes the room or chooses to stay in the dark room and fall back asleep.

You can modify this code to add more rooms, choices, and outcomes to create a more complex and interesting game. Text-based adventure games are a fun and creative way to practice programming and build interactive applications in Python.

Automating Tasks Using Python

Python's flexibility and ease of use make it a perfect tool for automating simple, repetitive tasks. With just a few lines of code, you can create custom scripts to automate tasks like managing files, sending emails, web scraping, and more.
Here are a few examples of simple tasks you can automate using Python:

Organizing Files: Python's os and shutil modules allow you to automate tasks like moving, renaming, or deleting files and directories. For example, you can write a script that automatically sorts your downloaded files into specific folders based on their file types.

```python
import os
import shutil

download_folder = '/path/to/your/download/folder'
images_folder = '/path/to/your/images/folder'
documents_folder = '/path/to/your/documents/folder'

for filename in os.listdir(download_folder):
    if filename.endswith('.jpg') or filename.endswith('.png'):
        shutil.move(os.path.join(download_folder, filename), images_folder)
    elif filename.endswith('.pdf') or filename.endswith('.docx'):
```

```python
        shutil.move(os.path.join(download_folder, filename), documents_folder)
```

Automating Web Scraping: Python's requests and BeautifulSoup modules make it easy to automate web scraping tasks, such as extracting data from a website and saving it to a local file.

```python
import requests
from bs4 import BeautifulSoup

url = 'https://example.com'
response = requests.get(url)
soup = BeautifulSoup(response.text, 'html.parser')
data = soup.find_all('div', class_='data-class')

with open('output.txt', 'w') as file:
    for item in data:
        file.write(item.text + '\n')
```

Sending Automated Emails: Python's smtplib and email modules can be used to send automated emails, such as sending daily reports or notifications.

```python
import smtplib
from email.mime.text import MIMEText

smtp_server = 'smtp.gmail.com'
smtp_port = 587
smtp_username = 'your_email@gmail.com'
smtp_password = 'your_password'
to_address = 'recipient@example.com'
subject = 'Automated Email'
message = 'This is an automated email sent from Python.'
```

```python
msg = MIMEText(message)
msg['From'] = smtp_username
msg['To'] = to_address
msg['Subject'] = subject

server = smtplib.SMTP(smtp_server, smtp_port)
server.starttls()
server.login(smtp_username, smtp_password)
server.sendmail(smtp_username, to_address, msg.as_string())
server.quit()
```

Automating Data Analysis: Python's pandas library allows you to automate data analysis tasks, such as importing data from spreadsheets or databases, cleaning and transforming the data, and creating visualizations.

```python
import pandas as pd

data = pd.read_csv('data.csv')
data = data.dropna()
data['total_sales'] = data['quantity'] * data['price']

sales_summary = data.groupby('product').agg({'total_sales': 'sum'})
sales_summary.to_excel('sales_summary.xlsx')
```

Automating simple tasks using Python can save you time and effort and help you accomplish more in less time. With a few lines of code, you can create custom scripts to automate tasks that would otherwise take hours to complete manually.

These are just a few examples of simple projects and applications you can create using Python. There are many more projects that you can explore and experiment with, depending on your interests and skill level. The key is to practice and apply what you've learned in real-world situations. Happy coding!

CHAPTER 15

DIVING DEEPER

As you've reached the end of this book, you should have a solid foundation in Python programming. However, the learning doesn't stop here. The world of Python is vast, and there are numerous libraries, frameworks, and tools available for you to explore. This chapter provides you with a roadmap for your next steps in Python programming and some resources to help you continue your learning journey.

Dive Deeper into Python Modules and Libraries:

NumPy and SciPy: These are the go-to libraries for numerical and scientific computing in Python. They provide tools for working with arrays, matrices, and advanced mathematical functions.

Pandas: This powerful data manipulation and analysis library provides easy-to-use data structures and tools for working with structured data.

Matplotlib and Seaborn: These libraries allow you to create beautiful and informative data visualizations in Python.

Scikit-learn: A machine learning library that provides tools for data analysis, modeling, and evaluation.

Explore Web Development with Python:
Flask: A lightweight web framework that allows you to quickly build web applications in Python.

Django: A robust web framework that provides a lot of built-in functionality for web development.

Web scraping: Learn how to extract data from websites using libraries like BeautifulSoup and Scrapy.

Get Started with Python for Data Science:

Machine Learning: Dive into the world of machine learning and explore various algorithms using libraries like scikit-learn and TensorFlow.

Data Analysis: Learn how to analyze large datasets using tools like Pandas and Jupyter Notebooks.

Data Visualization: Create compelling visualizations to help you understand and present your data using Matplotlib and Seaborn.

Automate Tasks and Create Scripts:

Automation: Python is great for automating repetitive tasks. Learn how to create scripts that can handle file management, data processing, and more.

Web scraping: Use Python to extract data from websites and store it in a usable format.

Learn Advanced Python Topics:

Metaclasses and Decorators: Explore the advanced features of Python that allow you to modify and extend the language itself.

Concurrency and Parallelism: Learn how to write Python code that can run on multiple threads or processes to increase performance.

Join the Python Community:

Online Forums and Discussion Boards: Engage with the Python community through online forums like Stack Overflow and Reddit's r/Python.

Python Conferences and Meetups: Attend Python-related conferences like PyCon or local Python meetups to learn from experts and network with other Python enthusiasts.

Remember, the key to becoming proficient in Python is consistent practice and exploration. Don't be afraid to try new things, break things, and learn from your mistakes. Keep exploring, keep coding, and keep learning!

Advanced Topics

Data science and machine learning are revolutionizing industries by enabling businesses to make data-driven decisions and create intelligent applications. Python is one of the most popular languages for data science and machine learning, thanks to its extensive libraries and user-friendly syntax. In this chapter, we'll discuss the role of Python in data science and machine learning, including its applications, libraries, and techniques.

Applications of Data Science and Machine Learning: Data science and machine learning have a wide range of applications.

As you gain experience in data science and machine learning with Python, explore advanced topics like deep learning, reinforcement learning, and ensemble methods.

Python's rich ecosystem of libraries and tools makes it an ideal language for data science and machine learning. With continuous learning and practice, you can harness the power of Python to extract insights from data, build predictive models, and create intelligent applications. Stay curious, keep experimenting, and you'll become a skilled data scientist or machine learning engineer in no time!

ABOUT THE AUTHOR

Anil Sharma, born to parents from a small village in India, migrated to the USA more than twenty years ago. He is a graduate of Electrical Engineering. He has been involved with automation and artificial intelligence for the last twenty-five years.